"This book will help you thrive in your marriage and beat the odds of divorce. The preventative information is the best I have ever seen, and the practical application covers it all. I have put *The Remarriage Checkup* at the top of my resource library for couples who find themselves in this beautiful and yet challenging world of remarriage."

Jim Burns, PhD
President, HomeWord
Author of *Creating an Intimate Marriage, Confident Parenting,* and *The Purity Code*

"This book is a must-read for any remarried couple. It includes the tools needed to create and maintain a wonderful remarriage."

From the Foreword by **Evelyn Husband Thompson**
Widow of Space Shuttle *Columbia* Commander Rick Husband
Now remarried to Bill Thompson

"With the high divorce rate among second and third marriages, this book is long overdue. Ron Deal and David Olson have done their homework, and what they have learned can help you beat the odds. It will take time and effort, but *The Remarriage Checkup* is the roadmap to a healthy marriage."

Gary D. Chapman, PhD
Author of *The Five Love Languages* and *Love As a Way of Life*

"Remarried or marrying again? Ron Deal and David Olson have a gift for you. This book is loaded with specific, useful ideas for helping your marriage reach its full potential. Using a combination of built-in assessment tools (and online tools if you want to go deeper), they will help you identify where you are at right now in your relationship. Drawing on surveys with 50,000 remarital couples, you will pinpoint your strengths and weaknesses and develop a realistic plan for having lasting love and joy in your marriage."

Scott Stanley, PhD
Author of *The Power of Commitment*
Research Professor, University of Denver

"Remarriages have unique challenges and different relational needs than first marriages. Based on a national study of 50,000 couples, this book is a wonderful resource for remarriage couples. Take the online Couple Checkup and get a report about your relationship, read the book, and build a relationship that lasts!"

Dr. Gary Smalley
Author of *The DNA of Relationships*

"The passion that Ron and David have for strengthening remarried couples is evident throughout this wonderfully crafted and easy-to-navigate tool. From the first page, you are drawn in and feel a sense of excitement and hopefulness. You are encouraged to be proactive and intentional about growing a strong, nurturing couple relationship and family. The recommendations are incredibly comprehensive and practical and are based on sound evidence from research on remarried couples. *The Remarriage Checkup* is the most up-to-date, relevant, complete guide for remarried couples—I know of no other resource like it. You will be educated, enlightened, and inspired."

Francesca Adler-Baeder, PhD
Associate Professor and Director, Center for Children, Youth, and Families, Auburn University
Director, National Stepfamily Resource Center

THE REMARRIAGE CHECKUP

TOOLS TO HELP YOUR MARRIAGE LAST A LIFETIME

Ron L. Deal, MMFT
David H. Olson, PhD

BETHANYHOUSE
MINNEAPOLIS, MINNESOTA

Published by Bethany House Publishers
11400 Hampshire Avenue South
Bloomington, Minnesota 55438

Bethany House Publishers is a division of
Baker Publishing Group, Grand Rapids, Michigan.

Printed in the United States of America

In keeping with biblical principles of creation stewardship, Baker Publishing Group advocates the responsible use of our natural resources. As a member of the Green Press Initiative, our company uses recycled paper when possible. The text paper of this book is comprised of 30% post-consumer waste.

green press INITIATIVE

Library of Congress Cataloging-in-Publication Data

Deal, Ron L.
    The remarriage checkup : tools to help your marriage last a lifetime / Ron L. Deal, David H. Olson.
        p.   cm.
    Includes bibliographical references.
    Summary: "Marriage and family experts explore the results of a national survey of over 50,000 remarrying couples, showing the keys to happy remarriage relationships. Readers can take an online survey, get personalized results, and see how their relationship compares. Includes discussion questions"—Provided by publisher.
    ISBN 978-0-7642-0758-7 (hardcover : alk. paper)   1. Remarriage.   2. Man-woman relationships.   3. Communication in marriage.   4. Conflict management.   I. Olson, David H. L. II. Title.
    HQ1018.D43   2010
    646.7'8—dc22

                                                                    2009040681

To all couples willing to risk again:

Love like you have nothing to lose.

About the Authors

Ron L. Deal, MMFT, is the founder of Successful Stepfamilies and an expert in remarriage and stepfamily education and therapy. He is the author of *The Smart Stepfamily* and coauthor with Laura Petherbridge of *The Smart Stepmom*. Ron is a licensed marriage and family therapist and licensed professional counselor who frequently appears in national media. He is a popular conference speaker and his video series *The Smart Stepfamily DVD* is used in communities, churches, and homes throughout the world. Ron is a member of the Stepfamily Expert Council for the National Stepfamily Resource Center. Ron and his wife, Nan, and their sons live in Amarillo, Texas.

For more about Ron Deal or to sign up for his free monthly newsletter, visit *www.SuccessfulStepfamilies.com*.

David H. Olson, PhD, is founder and president of Life Innovations, which produces a variety of products designed to build stronger marriages. A national and international marriage and family expert, Olson is professor emeritus at the University of Minnesota and the author of more than twenty books. Dr. Olson has appeared on a variety of television programs including *Today, The Early Show, Good Morning America,* and *Oprah.* He lives in suburban St. Paul, Minnesota.

For more about David Olson and the Couple Checkup and PRE-PARE/ENRICH Program, visit *www.PREPARE-ENRICH.com*.

Acknowledgments

FROM RON:

Every researcher stands on the shoulders of other researchers; good research paves a path for more. The landmark research behind this book is built on countless marital and family researchers (too many to list, I'm afraid), but mostly it is born out of the work of my coauthor, David H. Olson. An innovative family systems theorist, an author, and a researcher, Dr. Olson's lifelong dedication to helping families has equipped therapists and educators to be better helpers, and it has taught millions of couples throughout the world how to have a better relationship. It has been my honor (and candidly, my awe) to work with him on this project.

I also owe a tremendous debt of gratitude to Dr. Olson's team at Life Innovations. Amy, Peter, Matt, Shar, et al.—it's been fun being part of the Couple Checkup Research Team. Let's find another five years and do more research!

To my family team—Nan, Braden, Connor, and Brennan—you know I couldn't do this without you. You are my inspiration and joy. I love you.

Special thanks go to my agent, Chip MacGregor (you worked twice as hard on this one!); our editor, Ellen Chalifoux; and Bethany House Publishers. What a partnership!

Others who have encouraged this journey include Bill and Evelyn

Thompson, who have seen the darker side of life and still love like they have nothing to lose. It's an honor to know you.

And finally I'd like to acknowledge the thousands of remarried couples I have met over the last two decades through my live conference events, personal therapy, and Web page *www.SuccessfulStepfamilies.com*: Thank you for sharing your stories and life journeys with me. But most of all, thank you for inspiring me to love more deeply. Despite your loss and pain, you find a way to fight for love. Well done.

FROM DAVID:

Writing a book with another person can be challenging as you work to blend your ideas and writing styles. But working with Ron was a true pleasure, as he brings his years of experience with stepfamilies as well as a fluid and clear writing style. He also has an intellectual curiosity about research, which has helped crystallize our data analysis. He was a pleasure to collaborate with on this book.

I want to thank the team of professionals at Life Innovations who helped with the data analysis and critiquing of the book. They include Karen Olson (my partner and best critic), Amy Olson-Sigg (my daughter and an exceptional writer), Sharlene Fye (computer expert and master of data analysis), and Peter Larson (president of Life Innovations, who knows how to integrate clinical and research ideas).

This book would not have been written without the data from the 50,000 couples who took PREPARE-MC (Marriage with Children), a premarital relationship profile that is designed to help couples get their stepfamilies off to a great start. The data from their lives informed us about the strengths and challenges that stepfamilies face. We have learned from their experiences and integrated their insights into this book. We thank them and wish them well.

CONTENTS

Foreword

Congratulations! You are wisely seeking vital information concerning remarriage. Whether you are considering remarriage or have already remarried, this book will provide revelation derived from extensive research and profound insight. The results may surprise you. Some areas of remarriage are not too difficult, and yet there are many areas that are surprisingly challenging.

I was married to my college sweetheart for almost twenty-one years. He died tragically during the failed reentry of the space shuttle *Columbia* in February 2003. In an instant, I became a widow and a single mom.

Rick and I met in college and married after he completed pilot training in the Air Force. We both grew up in Amarillo, Texas. During our engagement, many showers and parties were given in our honor. We had dated five years before marrying, and it was a wonderful celebration.

Five years after Rick's death, I met the second love of my life, Bill Thompson. Our families were well acquainted with one another through church, and soon after his wife's death from cancer we began to date. Reactions were very mixed, unlike my experience with Rick. People were concerned about the very fast pace of our relationship. We fell deeply in love within months. We shared common spiritual beliefs and held the same values in life. I must admit that I found it difficult to understand why everyone was not overjoyed for us, considering our past experiences of pain and loss.

When Bill and I became engaged and announced it to my two children, the response consisted of one bursting into tears and the other sighing very deeply. No hearty congratulations like the first time around. My mom was happy for me, yet very guarded in her congratulations.

Any remarriage begins with an adjustment and recognition that there has been a loss. Our hearts were full of joy, yet we have had to learn that others were struggling with a significant change. Our joy seemed to magnify the loss of others.

The great news is that it is not a permanent condition. My mom grew to absolutely love Bill before her untimely death in May 2009. My children have grown to love Bill very much also; yet they still remember, miss, and treasure memories of their dad. Ron Deal has been an inspiration and a godsend to our family with his insight into the mechanics of a stepfamily.

Remarriages are more complicated than first marriages. Children are already in the picture. Patterns for communication, attitudes toward work vs. leisure time, financial goals (including spending/saving), and spiritual beliefs are much more deep-seated.

This book is a must-read for any remarried couple. It includes the tools needed to create and maintain a wonderful remarriage. These pages identify areas you may or may not have considered important, but together with the online Couple Checkup you will learn all the strengths and weaknesses you possess individually and as a couple.

Having experienced cancer with both of my parents, and Bill with his first wife, we know that diagnostic tests are used to determine the best course of treatment. Similarly, the online Couple Checkup will guide you through the labyrinth of relationships inside a remarriage.

I am excited for you because you will grow and learn so much from *The Remarriage Checkup*. May you be mightily blessed and strengthened with all the tools this great book will provide for you, and may God bless your family!

—Evelyn Husband Thompson,
  Widow of Space Shuttle *Columbia*
  Commander Rick Husband
  Now remarried to Bill Thompson

Discover Your
Couple Positioning System (CPS)

New technology in the last decade has made GPS or Global Positioning Systems accessible to nearly everyone around the world. A businessperson traveling in an unfamiliar city can use a GPS device in her rental car to find her destination. Explorers can use GPS guidance to determine where they are on the earth's surface and where they must go to find their hidden treasure.

What if you had a CPS—a Couple Positioning System—that helped you determine the strengths of your relationship (i.e., your "current location") and helped you know where to look for hidden treasures? Congratulations, you've just picked it up.

This book provides a map for couples on the unique journey of remarriage. It reveals findings from the National Survey of Couples Creating Stepfamilies, the largest study of remarrying couples with children from previous relationships ever conducted. We examined the profiles of over 50,000 couples (over 100,000 people) to discover the qualities that best predict highly satisfying relationships and the roadblocks couples must overcome in order to beat the odds of divorce.

Some of our findings will validate what you already know about successful relationships; others will surprise you. Reading this book will guide you into a more intimate remarriage relationship.

Even though our study was of premarital couples about to form stepfamilies, the results have broad application to all remarried and stepfamily couples. Even before marriage the difference between high-quality relationships and low-quality ones is evident and predicts later marital success. Our national survey of couples was based on their responses to PREPARE-MC (Marriage with Children), a premarital relationship strengths inventory. Previous studies (with a related assessment called PREPARE) have found that the strengths and issues couples have before marriage are highly predictive of their relationship after the wedding. In fact, in three longitudinal studies where we followed couples for an extended period of time we found that their PREPARE scores before marriage predicted with 80 to 85 percent accuracy which couples would be happily married and which couples would be separated/divorced after three years. These studies demonstrate that what happens before marriage is highly predictive of success after becoming married. This research also validates our clinical experience, which tells us that many of the dynamics that eventually divide remarried couples—even after many years of marriage—began early in their relationship. Therefore, whether you are currently dating or looking to improve your marriage, the findings in this book are for you.

Further, when combined with a personalized assessment of the condition of your relationship (received after taking the online Couple Checkup), the secrets revealed in this book become even more illuminating. You will know when to feel confident in your relationship and what must improve to avoid disaster.

WHAT EXACTLY IS A COUPLE CHECKUP?

The Couple Checkup is an online assessment of twenty relationship areas that have been found to be significant for dating, engaged, and married couples. Based on the popular and highly successful PREPARE/ENRICH Program, the Couple Checkup is being used throughout the world. The Couple Checkup is founded on over twenty-five years of research on couples using the PREPARE/ENRICH Program (used by over 2.5 million couples). Numerous studies have demonstrated the scientific rigor of the program for premarital and married couples and for couples from various ethnic backgrounds.

Benefits of the Online Couple Checkup:

The seven letters in the word *checkup* can help you remember the advantages of taking the Checkup with your partner.

- **C — Create positive change:** You can create positive changes in your relationship by establishing new habits that promote a more satisfying relationship. The Couple Checkup will help bring new ideas to your relationship.

- **H — Healthy for your relationship:** Checkups promote and maintain health. Just like a physical or dental checkup provides information that can motivate behavior change, the Couple Checkup promotes healthier decisions and behavior in your relationship.

- **E — Evaluate where you are now:** Identify your current relationship strengths and problems, and then make a plan for growing your relationship.

- **C — Communicate more effectively:** The Checkup gives you the opportunity and structure for having productive discussions.

- **K — Kick-start your relationship:** Completing the Checkup primes you to think and talk with your partner in helpful ways.

- **U — Understand each other:** You will better know and understand your partner after taking the online Couple Checkup. You may be surprised to learn how your partner feels about many aspects of your relationship.

- **P — Proactive versus reactive:** Too often couples wait for a crisis before they deal with a problematic situation. By being proactive, you will be better able to take control of your relationship and make it more satisfying for both of you.

IS THE COUPLE CHECKUP RELEVANT TO US?

The Couple Checkup is designed to be relevant for couples who are dating, engaged, and married. As you take the online Couple Checkup, it tailors itself specifically to your couple stage, your age, and the parenting circumstances of your relationship (biological children and/or stepchildren). Based on your answers, the computer system will select relevant questions and scales for your relationship. Whether dating, engaged, or already married, your inventory is tailor-made to your specific type of relationship.

You do not have to take the online Couple Checkup to read and apply this book. But to discover the hidden treasures in your relationship, we highly recommend that you do. Look inside the dust cover of this book for your online voucher code and get one free personal profile. This code also provides significant savings off the retail price when your dating or married partner takes the Checkup as well. Both of you must take the profile to receive the comprehensive Couple Report identifying your strengths and growth areas.

Take the Online Couple Checkup

Get one free Individual Report at *www.couplecheckup.com* by using the voucher code provided inside the dust cover of this book. This code also provides a significant discount on the purchase of the full Couple Checkup (when your partner also takes the profile) that compares you and your partner and provides a comprehensive Couple Checkup Report.

Chapter 1

Checkup and Check-in

Is it wise to let your car go 100,000 miles before getting an oil change?

Would you tell your children to get a dental cleaning only once every twenty-five years?

Is a physical or cardiogram advisable only once in your lifetime?

The answer to all three questions is no. Regular checkups on your car and proactive care of your body are generally practiced activities. Yet dating and married couples rarely, if ever, do a checkup on their relationship even though a relationship checkup can help them experience a happier and more successful relationship. The sooner you identify issues unique to your relationship and find ways to resolve them, the easier it will be to create a stronger couple relationship. And the sooner you discover your relationship strengths and build on them, the deeper and more intimate your relationship will be.

Don and Jennifer[1] missed a number of checkup points, and their relationship suffered because of it. When first married, their inability to effectively resolve conflict didn't seem like such a big deal. Don often ended up feeling responsible for the problem, while Jennifer didn't feel that she could find a way to help Don really understand her opinions and ideas. Instead of working on their problem-solving skills, they chose to avoid and deny the touchy subjects that led to conflict. Problems would temporarily go away, but what Don and Jennifer didn't know was that the accumulation of small, unresolved arguments was seeding resentment in their relationship. A checkup would have raised a warning flag, but they never took the time.

Over a period of time, the conflicts in their relationship escalated, especially those over Don's children. Don was willing to avoid touchy issues when it pertained to him, but he wasn't willing to look away from issues that troubled his children. The more Jennifer and his children collided, the more he felt the need to defend them. Soon Jennifer's resentment of his children grew, and the small disagreements they could once overlook were larger than hope. Eventually the couple no longer felt close or connected. Their unresolved anger and hurt drove them apart, affecting their sex life and communication.

By contrast, Wes and Ann regularly engaged in activities that led them to evaluate the condition of their marriage. They attended marriage classes at least once a year and talked with other couples who wanted better marriages. Because Wes was on a retreat-planning committee at his church, he and Ann took the online Couple Checkup to become familiar with it. (They thought it might be helpful to others.) What they discovered is that each had growing concerns about an aspect of their marriage that the other didn't know about. Because the report provided them early detection, they were able to talk through the matters and move beyond them.

Early detection and prevention is one key to building stronger marriages. If couples would take an annual checkup and learn about their strengths and small issues that are hidden below the surface, there would be fewer divorces because smaller issues would be eliminated; molehills would not become mountains. If uncovered problems turn out to be serious, they could go to marital therapy as early as possible rather than waiting till a crisis erupts.

This book and the online Couple Checkup could provide you early detection against potentially problematic issues. Just as important, it could also affirm the strengths and qualities that currently comprise your relationship and help you to build an even stronger marriage.

THE DIRECTIONAL FLOW OF YOUR RELATIONSHIP

Much like a river flowing over thousands of miles from its source to its final destination, marriage flows through the ever-changing passages of our lives. On the surface, a marriage may look relatively stable, but deeper examination reveals undercurrents that form the heart and soul of the relationship. The water volume of a river creates force as it flows, enabling it to cut a path or direction; likewise, the qualities of your marriage have the power to determine its course and the ease with which it flows.

The Mississippi River is the second-longest river in North America. Though it begins at Lake Itasca in northern Minnesota, watershed from thirty-one U.S. states and two Canadian provinces contributes to the river before it empties into the Gulf of Mexico, some 2,320 miles later. Your marriage will also change over time with the addition and launching of children, changes in family and work responsibilities, individual and relational crises that complicate life, and changes in your personal emotional maturity.

But these challenges can also cause your relationship to lose volume as they drain your time and energy levels. That's why replenishment is crucial to a happy partnership. This can come in a variety of ways, many of which are already present in your relationship—we call them strengths (we will help you identify and build on these strengths); others will need to be developed over time. Dating, courtship, and a wedding are the "source" of a relationship. But how a marriage sustains itself throughout the ebb and flow of life is what deepens and strengthens the undercurrents of the relationship.

CHECKING IN

Jean was trying to find a way to "check in" with her husband. She was feeling a bit distant from Tom, who had become extra involved with work. She began reading this book and taking the online Couple Checkup; she was not able to finish the Checkup before picking up her daughter from a piano lesson. When she got home, Tom was relaxing, watching television after a hectic day. She told Tom about the Checkup, but he did not seem very interested. She said, "Just try it and see what you think." Reluctantly Tom took the Checkup and then Jean finished hers. Just a few minutes later they received an email notice that their Couple Report was ready to be printed.

Both were curious about the results and were pleasantly surprised by the fact that they had more strengths as a couple than they expected. In addition, Tom noticed that Jean was not happy with their communication and both were unhappy about how they managed their finances. The report reminded them that they had grown up in very different families, and they saw how some of those differences still impact them today. Both chuckled when the report showed that Jean was more organized than Tom (they already discovered that the hard way).

While Tom started out somewhat reluctant to take the Checkup, he found himself very involved in the discussion and was surprised by how much he learned. Jean also felt there were now many more things they could discuss in the future, and she felt more connected and hopeful after discussing their results.

Jean and Tom used our 3-step Couple Positioning System to help them learn and grow from their Couple Report. As you read this book, you too can use this process to help apply what you will learn in each chapter.

1. Where are you NOW? (Identify and Discuss Your Results)
First, you and your partner should read through this book, perhaps one chapter at a time. Then review your individual and couple results from the Checkup Report that coincides with the chapter you have just read. In addition to the general advice given in this book, reviewing your report will give you specific information and ideas about how each chapter applies to your marriage.

Keep in mind that with all individual scores, one of you may be more satisfied with that aspect of your marriage than the other. Talk about your own perspective and listen to your partner's. (Don't try to read each other's minds about why you are or are not satisfied with a given dimension of your relationship.)

2. Where would you like to be? (Discuss Issues) Next, you and your partner will discuss how satisfied you are with each aspect of your relationship. You will be given the opportunity to applaud your strengths and improve less-than-satisfying aspects.

3. How do you get there? (Develop Your Action Plan) While discussions are helpful, there comes a point when you need to take action to grow and increase your relationship satisfaction. Based on your discussions, you will want to live out some of your ideas and decisions by putting them into practice. Also, this is a great way to practice new skills.

ENJOY THE PROCESS OF BUILDING A HEALTHIER RELATIONSHIP!

Now it's time for you to work through your first check-in process. Remember, it's up to you to apply the principles of this book and learn from your personal Couple Checkup Report. Together they might affirm what's healthy in your relationship or point out a matter that needs your attention, but they can't make you grow. Only you can do that. Will the process be risky? Perhaps. But that risk can bring great reward!

COUPLE POSITIONING SYSTEM (CPS)

Where are you NOW? (Identify and Discuss Your Results)

Beginning with the next chapter, you will review and discuss your individual and couple results. For now, discuss the following questions as you begin your journey to enhance your relationship. Consider each privately to yourself. Then listen to your partner's perspective, being sure you fully understand before offering your own.

- All couples have periods of time when they are proactively looking after their marriage (like Wes and Ann, p. 18) and times when they get blindsided by stress or difficulties (like Don and Jennifer). In the last six months would you say you've been more proactive or reactive? Share your thoughts with your partner (and remember to take time to listen and give validity to your partner's ideas as well).
- Early detection of cancer and dental cavities makes perfect sense to most people. What, in your opinion, keeps couples from taking the time for early detection of marital strain?
- Review the Benefits of the Couple Checkup section on page 15. Share which of these you are most looking forward to and why. Take turns sharing and listening.
- If you haven't taken the online Couple Checkup yet, what logistical reasons have held you back (e.g., not enough free time, computer is not connected to the Internet)? What relationship matters have prohibited you from taking it (e.g., concerned about what the report might say, anger in the marriage)?
- What are you most curious to learn from the Couple Checkup Report?

Where would you like to be? (Discuss Issues)

a. Identify Issues
- What do you find uncomfortable about talking through this Couple Positioning System process?

- What aspects of your life sometimes get in the way of nurturing your relationship?
- What stumbling blocks need to be removed?

b. Resolve Issues

- Discuss how the above issues might be managed while you begin reading this book and exploring your relationship.

How do you get there? (Develop Your Action Plan)

a. If you have not taken the online Couple Checkup yet, commit to a time and place to complete the inventory.

b. If you have taken the Checkup, agree to a game plan:

- Decide how and when you will read the book. Will you share the book or read together? Some couples enjoy reading each chapter independently and highlighting what they find interesting or helpful. Choose different colors so you can look back to see what each of you found most important.

- Decide on a weekly or bimonthly meeting time and place where you will work through the Couple Positioning System process for each chapter. Be sure to pace yourself and not try to swallow the entire book at once. We strongly encourage you to join other couples for a group study of the book. Church and community groups may want to use our Small Group Discussion Guide available at *www.SuccessfulStepfamilies.com* and *www.CoupleCheckup.com*.

Chapter 2

Building on Your Strengths

The need that offers the greatest potential for joy is also the need that offers the greatest potential for pain, the need to share our life with someone.

—Javan,
Twentieth-century American poet

Adara found herself in the paradox of marriage. "I love Juan more than anything in the world and yet he drives me crazy sometimes. There are just some things I find hard to respect about him. How is it that I can be drawn so passionately to someone who makes me loco?"

Marriage can be a source of great joy but also a source of great frustration. If you've already begun your Couple Positioning System discussions, you may have experienced warmth and closeness and disagreement and feelings of discomfort—all in the same conversation! Within marriage, individuals can have a source of happiness and a haven from the rest of the world. But marriage can also affect partners negatively, making them feel as if they need to retreat from each other. The challenge is to make marriage a mutually satisfying relationship, and one that works well over time. To accomplish this, you must build on your strengths.

WHY LOVE IS NOT ENOUGH

"Love is all you need." "Love makes the world go round." "Love means never having to say you're sorry." So much has been written about love—especially the romantic feelings of love—that there is an overemphasis on the passions that drive us together. Although love is indeed a powerful emotion, it is idealistic to think that passion is all you need. The feelings of love alone are not enough to make a marriage work. How do we know this? Most Americans report being in love at the time of marriage, yet the overall divorce rate still continues to be about 50 percent, and as you'll see in chapter 3, the divorce rate for remarried coupless is even higher.

In addition, frequently one person in a couple is much happier than their partner. In fact, there is a low correlation in marital satisfaction between spouses, meaning that if you know the satisfaction level of one partner, you will only be able to predict the other partner's marital satisfaction 25 percent of the time.

Susan's feelings toward her husband, Terry, fluctuated from warm and close to questioning whether they could ever be truly happy. She sometimes wondered if they were on the same page, especially when they went through a period with almost no communication. The drought, as she called it, really bothered her. But Terry didn't seem to mind being disconnected. In fact, it didn't seem to bother him even if they did not communicate very much for several days—at least as far as she could tell. She assumed this meant that Terry did not really love her or care how she felt.

Many unhappy couples stay married because they feel it is too upsetting to get divorced. These couples have very little vitality left in their relationship. We've all seen this dynamic played out when noticing a couple in a restaurant who rarely talks during the entire meal. You can just tell there isn't much life in their marriage.

COMPARING HAPPY AND UNHAPPY COUPLES

So why is it that some couples seem so happy, regardless of life situations, transitions, or circumstances they may encounter, and others don't? Are they simply well-matched individuals? Are they doing something different from less-happy couples? What is their secret?

Our study of over 50,000 couples revealed a list of the top strengths of vibrant stepcouples. (The online Couple Checkup will allow you to see how your relationship compares.) The top five strengths clearly distinguish great relationships from unsatisfying ones and are detailed in the chart Five Keys to Intimacy. Relationship satisfaction is highly impacted first and foremost by the personality of each partner. The

Five Keys to Intimacy:
Happy vs. Unhappy Couples

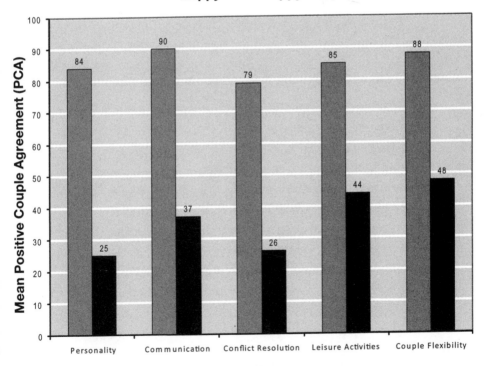

Happy Couples (n=15,056)   Unhappy Couples (n=15,433)

"likability" factor, as we might call it, of each person is critical to marital satisfaction. Partners who are jealous, withdrawn, stubborn, critical, and/or controlling are not very likable. Needless to say, they have less satisfying marriages.

Other important factors that strengthen and protect the couple's relationship include healthy communication, the couple's ability to resolve conflict, sharing leisure activities together, and the ability to be flexible in their approach to life. These qualities are so critical to relationship success that an entire chapter will be dedicated to each in order to help you incorporate them into your relationship.

Besides these highly significant five factors, there were five more in our survey that were strong indicators of couple satisfaction. These ten factors are able to predict with 90 percent accuracy whether couples were highly satisfied or unhappy in their relationship.

═══ Key Strengths of Highly Satisfied Remarriage Couples ═══

1. Satisfaction with and acceptance of the personality of your partner.
2. Healthy communication.
3. An ability to resolve couple conflict.
4. Shared couple leisure activity.
5. Strong couple flexibility and adaptability.
6. Good financial management and shared values for handling money.
7. Healthy sexuality and affection within the relationship.
8. Positive shared friendships and healthy boundaries with extended family that support the couple.
9. Successful management of the complexities of living in a stepfamily.
10. Positive couple closeness and emotional safety.

IDENTIFYING AND OVERCOMING COMMON STUMBLING BLOCKS

Our national sample of over 50,000 couples also revealed the most common problematic issues for stepcouples. An issue was identified when couples disagreed about an item or when the couple agreed that the stated issue was indeed a problem for them. We determined both the most problematic relationship categories and the most problematic specific issues stepcouples face. Our in-depth analysis discovered that the twelve most anticipated problem areas for remarriage couples come from six general relationship categories: marriage expectations and relationship concerns; children, parenting, and stepparenting; finances and debt; personality issues; conflict resolution; and communication. Specific issues within those categories are listed below with the percent of all couples experiencing them.

=========== **Remarriage Stumbling Blocks** ===========

Items are in Rank Order
1. They expect difficulty dealing with complex stepfamily issues. (88%)
2. They believe having children from previous relationships will put an additional strain on their marriage. (86%)
3. Creating a stepfamily puts more stress on their relationship. (85%)
4. Having different patterns of childrearing in their birth family can be problematic. (82%)
5. They expect stepfamily adjustment to be difficult. (78%)
6. They don't have a specific plan for money management. (73%)
7. They have concerns over unpaid bills, debts, or settlements. (66%)
8. They feel their partner is too stubborn. (65%)
9. One or both of the partners goes out of their way to avoid conflict with the other. (63%)
10. They have a fear of another marital failure. (63%)

11. One or both partners feel responsible for the problems when they argue. (61%)
12. One or both partners have not yet worked through the issues and hurts from previous relationships. (58%)

Notice how many of the stumbling blocks pertain to the complexity of marriage in a stepfamily and the couple's past. Four of the top five issues specifically deal with stepfamily concerns. One of the two money issues is related to the couple's past, and two additional issues (the fear of relationship failure and resolving hurts from the past) also relate to previous relationships. In all, seven of the top twelve specific issues for remarriage couples relate to the resolution of their past or the complexity of their stepfamily present. This makes it clear that overcoming these issues is a critical part of couple success.

It is worthy to note that 88 percent of remarriage couples expect to have difficulties with stepfamily issues. But expecting difficulties and knowing how to manage them are two different things. Our clinical experience shows that despite an awareness that stepfamily issues will prove problematic for their marriage, most couples don't fully anticipate the magnitude of the stressors they will face and often are not equipped to deal with it.

We should also mention that several of these common problem issues are faced by healthy and unhealthy couples alike. Some couples, however, are better able to resolve or cope with them. One of our goals is to help you not only identify your issues, but learn how to move beyond them.

TURN YOUR STUMBLING BLOCKS INTO STEPPING-STONES

"The block of granite, which is an obstacle on the path of the weak, becomes a stepping-stone on the path of the strong."

Thomas Carlyle (1795–1881)

The only difference between stumbling blocks and stepping-stones is how we choose to use them. In other words, something that we perceive as an obstacle in our life can be overcome by simply changing the way we look at it.

A father and son went on a hike to find the source of a historic freshwater spring. The father, slowed by middle age, struggled to keep up with his agile young son, who bounded through the woods in excitement. They discovered the spring and decided to get closer to the source opening in the side of the mountain, but large rocks blocked their path. As the father stood contemplating how they might work around the boulders, without hesitation his son climbed a rock and began bounding from one to another. The father called to his son to be careful, but quickly noticed that what was a barrier to him had become a stepping-stone to his son. And if he wanted to keep up, he too would have to find a way to turn this obstacle into a path.

Relationships are dynamic and changing. Many factors can propel your relationship into either positive or negative change, including life cycle stages, time, and events or behaviors within or outside of the relationship. By reading this book and applying the information to your life, you can improve your relationship, regardless of the problems you may have.

All of your choices and actions will have some kind of result. Motivational speaker Les Brown said, "If you want to keep on getting what you're getting, keep on doing what you're doing." But if you want to achieve something different, you and your partner both must be willing to do something different. Many couples who want changes make the mistake of using the same approach over and over, and they keep getting the same result. Listen to your partner and your own needs, and take new steps to make your partnership more mutually satisfying.

"You can't stop the waves, but you can learn to surf."

Jon Kabat-Zinn

Understanding the differences and obstacles in our relationships removes some of the power they have over us. Awareness generates in us the ability to maneuver more intelligently, perhaps by confronting the challenge that these stumbling blocks pose rather than tripping over them. The following is a good example of how to turn your stumbling blocks (weaknesses) into stepping-stones (strengths).

A ten-year-old boy decided to study judo despite the fact that he had lost his left arm in a devastating car accident. The boy began lessons with an old Japanese judo master. The boy was doing well, so he couldn't understand why, after three months of training, the master had taught him only one move. "Sensei," the boy finally said, "shouldn't I be learning more moves?"

"This is the only move you know, but this is the only move you'll ever need to know," the sensei replied. Not quite understanding, but trusting in his teacher, the boy kept training.

Several months later, the sensei took the boy to his first tournament. Surprising himself, the boy easily won his first two matches. The third match proved to be more difficult, but after some time, his opponent became impatient and charged; the boy deftly used his one move to win the match. Still amazed by his success, the boy was now in the finals.

This time his opponent was bigger, stronger, and more experienced. For a while, the boy appeared to be overmatched. Concerned that the boy might get hurt, the referee called a time-out. He was about to stop the match when the sensei intervened. "No," the sensei insisted, "let him continue."

Soon after the match resumed, his opponent made a critical mistake: He dropped his guard. Instantly, the boy used his move to pin him. The boy had won the match and the tournament. He was a champion.

On the way home, the boy and the sensei reviewed every move in each match. Then the boy summoned the courage to ask what was really on his mind.

"Sensei, how did I win the tournament with only one move?"

"You won for two reasons," the sensei answered. "First, you've almost mastered one of the most difficult throws in all of judo. And second, the only known defense for that move is for your opponent to grab your left arm."

The boy's biggest weakness had become his biggest strength.

—Bits and Pieces[1]

The online Couple Checkup can help you identify some of your stumbling blocks (issues). Knowing and discussing your stumbling blocks enables you to find ways to turn them into strengths. Our Couple Positioning System process is designed to help you identify your strengths as a couple and the issues in your relationship that cause you to "stumble"—to lose some of your original vitality and energy (Where are you NOW?). You are encouraged to discuss an issue (Where do you want to be?) and then develop an action plan to implement solutions (How do you get there?).

Our goal is to empower you and your partner to build on your strengths. The things that brought you together can help you build a more vital and mutually satisfying relationship.

In Everyone's Life . . .

In everyone's life there are problems to solve,
Even in the strongest relationship,
there are differences to overcome.

It is easy to give up when confronted with difficulties;
to fool yourself into believing that
perfection can be found somewhere else.

But true happiness and a lasting relationship are found
when you look inside yourself
for solutions to the problems.

Instead of walking away when things get tough
and blaming the other person,
look for compromise and forgiveness.

Caring is not a matter of convenience.
It is a commitment of one soul to another.

THE REMARRIAGE CHECKUP

And if each gives generously of themselves,
then both lives are enriched.

The problems will come and go,
just like the changing seasons.
But unselfish love is constant and everlasting.

—Susan Staszewski

COUPLE EXERCISE

Identifying Couple Strengths and Growth Areas

1. Look at the list below and identify **3 areas** that you consider a **Strength (S)** in your relationship and mark them with an S. Let each partner make their own determinations.

2. Then identify **3 areas** that you think could use some improvement, which we call a **Growth Area (G)**, and mark them with a G.

	Strength Area (S)	Growth Area (G)
Expectations (pre-marital only)	_____	_____
Communication	_____	_____
Conflict Resolution	_____	_____
Financial Management	_____	_____
Affection & Sexuality	_____	_____
Spiritual Beliefs	_____	_____
Roles in Your Relationship	_____	_____
Family & Friends	_____	_____

3. Now do the Couple Positioning System process with your partner:

*(Turn to the "**Summary of Strength and Growth Areas**" page of your Couple Checkup Report)*

COUPLE POSITIONING SYSTEM (CPS)

Where are you NOW? (Identify and Discuss Your Results)

a. Review the Couple Checkup Couple Results.

- What are they? Keep in mind that your strengths are couple strengths, which means that you both agree (high couple agreement) that a given area is a positive aspect of your relationship. If only one of you is satisfied with that aspect of your relationship, it will not be a true couple strength and will be reflected by a moderate or low score.

- Did your list from item 2 match the Couple Checkup analysis?

b. Discuss your Relationship Strengths.

- Our survey of couples included 165 statements. The following statements were most predictive of success. In fact, how couples responded to these statements can predict with over 90 percent accuracy whether relationships are healthy and satisfying or unhappy. Would you agree or disagree with each statement?

======= **Top Ten Statements Predicting Health** =======

Items are in order of how closely they relate to couple satisfaction.

1. One partner's moodiness is not an issue in our relationship.
2. Each of us feels understood by the other.
3. We are able to resolve our differences.
4. We enjoy many of the same leisure activities.
5. We are creative in how we handle our differences.
6. We agree on how to spend money.
7. Affection is used fairly in our relationship and sexuality is healthy.
8. Neither of us is overly involved or influenced by his/her family or previous partner.
9. We have worked out parent and stepparent responsibilities and roles.
10. Each of us feels close to the other.

c. On your Couple Report, note your Couple Type—you will learn more about this in chapter 4.

- If your Couple Type is Conflicted or Devitalized, don't be discouraged at this point. Admit that there is work to be done and trust that change is possible. If your relationship does not improve as you continue to work through the book and exercises, you may want to consult a licensed marriage therapist who can help you overcome your barriers.

Where would you like to be? (Discuss Issues)

a. You will learn much more about these relationship aspects (and others) throughout this book. For now, discuss which Growth Areas you most want to improve. These are areas you can pay special attention to as you work through the book.
b. Be sure to listen to the other person's identified Growth Area.

How do you get there? (Develop Your Action Plan)

a. Don't get ahead of the book. You may be tempted right now to go to work trying to change something in your relationship. Be patient and let each chapter guide your growth process.
b. Renew your commitment to working through the book together.

Chapter 3

Beating the Odds of Divorce: The Stepfamily Connection

Strong marriages don't just happen. They are created over time by the intentional effort of the couple. Like the painter's masterpiece, building a healthy marriage requires skill, creativity, endurance, and a working knowledge of the canvas, brush, and paint.

—Ron L. Deal

We went to counseling at our church prior to getting married because we knew it was not going to be an easy transition. It has turned out to be far tougher than I imagined.

—Remarried two years;
Father of two, stepfather of one

THE CHALLENGING JOURNEY FOR STEP-FAMILIES

Happily ever after. It doesn't sound like too much to ask for. But there is a significant gap between those who seek and those who find. A quick look at marriage in America reveals that nearly half of all marriages don't survive, let alone become safe, supportive, and loving relationships. An additional 25 percent of all marriages that don't end in divorce are dissatisfying—*unhappily ever after.*[1] Certainly these couples didn't marry with the expectation of divorce or distress. So what went wrong? And more to the point, what will keep you and your spouse from crashing and burning beside them?

In general, remarriages (where one or both partners have been married before) with or without children have a 60 percent or greater chance of divorce. Specifically, second marriages have a 60 percent divorce rate and third marriages a 73 percent chance of divorce.[2] Remarried couples who bring children to the wedding have an even greater risk of divorce; to be specific, they have a 50 percent greater chance of divorce than remarried couples without children.[3] As it turns out, happily ever after is tougher to achieve in remarriage, even more difficult when one of you brings children to the marriage, and especially challenging when you both do. That's why we conducted this specific study on remarriage and why we wrote this book—to help you beat the odds and break the cycle of divorce for you and your children. Before you get too discouraged, know that the qualities of successful remarried and stepfamily couples are identifiable—*and you can learn them and use them in your marriage.* This book will tell you how to be successful and will equip you with the tools to get there. The journey to happily ever after begins here.

Every journey will have a few surprises along the way. If you've ever experienced an airline delay or cancellation, you know exactly what we mean. If bad weather rolls in or your plane is missing a windshield wiper, you're stuck in Timbuktu for the night. But the difference between people who become overly stressed by unforeseen circumstances and those who thrive in them is the ability to adapt. Such persons are able to discern what they cannot change from what they can control and then make the appropriate adjustments. Others, however, get plowed over by the out-of-control circumstances and fall apart. No doubt you've seen people scream at an airline ticket agent because their flight had been cancelled due to inclement weather.

The agent couldn't be held responsible, but he or she nevertheless ended up the target of someone's frustration.

Similarly, the remarriage journey has plenty of surprises along the way. Indeed, if all of your marital and stepfamily expectations came about just as you dreamed, there wouldn't be any "delays" or "cancellations." Your marriage and family would come together just fine, and without much work on your part. But the reality of remarriage is that life in a stepfamily is much more difficult than most couples anticipate. The unique challenges of being a stepcouple work against marital success, and only those who intentionally work to overcome them find the rewards they dreamed of before walking down the aisle.

STEPCOUPLES: REMARRIED WITH CHILDREN

Stepcouple is the word we will use throughout this book to describe a couple whose marriage was preceded by the birth of at least one child to at least one of the partners (in a previous relationship). The term *stepcouple* also accurately communicates our conviction that marriage in a stepfamily cannot be enhanced without consideration of the entire stepfamily system. One cannot compartmentalize the couple's relationship as if it exists in a vacuum. In other words, the health of the couple's relationship is interdependent with the health of the stepfamily. Each greatly impacts the other.

Tim, a stepfather of three, said, "The only problem is that I discovered this truth too late. We have been having problems for some time now, mostly about her kids." Tim felt that the conflicts between him and his wife over one particular child led to a divorce that he couldn't prevent. "I guess I got whooped by a nine-year-old," he said. Children—and the other unique aspects of stepfamily life—have everything to do with the success of your marriage.

The average stepfamily has many people in the extended family system, and each person is required to manage a multitude of relationships. Because of this, Drs. John and Emily Visher, founders of the Stepfamily Association of America, joked for many years that stepfamilies don't have a family tree—they have a family forest! Stepcouples can easily get lost in the stepfamily forest. Before marriage, pre-stepfamily couples are often very intentional about their relationship and may spend a great deal of time together without the children. But once the wedding takes place and real life sets in, many stepcouples get lost in a sea of activities, child-rearing responsibilities, divided loyalties, and relational concerns.

Our study validated what we have believed for some time. A couple's previous marriages (or relationships) and the presence of stepchildren have a significant impact on the long-term viability of the remarriage, but the full weight of this impact doesn't show up until *after* the wedding. Before the wedding, matters related to ex-spouses and stepparenting had limited impact on the couple's level of satisfaction with each other. However, after the wedding, stepfamily issues rose significantly in their impact on couple satisfaction.[4] This finding is very important because it points out how marriage in a stepfamily is different.

In a first marriage, the couple's relationship forms the basis for family stability; it becomes the foundation of the home. Furthermore, the health of the marriage supports and facilitates the parent-child relationships that follow. However, in stepfamilies, the complexities of stepfamily living dramatically impact the couple just as the couple impacts how stepfamily matters are handled. For example, the stepparent-stepchild relationship(s) can determine the success of the couple; so can how a former spouse (and even *their* new spouse) interacts with the new family or how children adjust to their parent's remarriage. All of these dynamics greatly influence the stepcouple's stability and overall happiness. In short, *remarriage is not just about the couple; it is also about their past and their children's present.* These stepfamily factors create stress in the home, which in turn "thickens the blood" of biological family members. Ultimately, this creates distress and distance in a couple's relationship.

WORKING SMARTER AS A COUPLE

In the book *The Smart Stepfamily: Seven Steps to a Healthy Family,* Ron points out that most stepcouples work hard at bringing together the members of their home. However, due to misguided assumptions about how to best make this happen, most stepcouples find themselves working hard, harder, and harder at bringing their family together, but often inadvertently in the wrong manner. The trick to building a successful stepfamily is not working harder, it's working smarter!

"It shouldn't have to be this much work," said Frank. "If your kids and I can't get along naturally, then maybe we shouldn't have gotten together in the first place." What this well-intentioned stepfather didn't realize is that integrating a stepfamily is indeed hard work. To expect otherwise is unrealistic. In fact, what is "natural" in a stepfamily is for new relationships to be undefined and strained from time to time. Frank's expectation for quick family harmony led him to make pressuring remarks to his wife like the one quoted above. Instead of pressuring expectations, he and she would be much better off learning smarter ways of building harmony.

"SO WHERE'S THE HONEYMOON?"

When presenting seminars for couples in stepfamilies, Ron often jokes with his audience that for stepcouples, the honeymoon comes at the end of the journey, not at the beginning. The fantasy of marital peace and harmony that leads couples to the altar usually doesn't become reality for seven or more years for most stepcouples.[5] (Some lucky couples with small children may discover the honeymoon within a few years.) Until then, it is hard work and determination—one step at a time—that finally pays off in a "honeymoon" experience. One stepmom, Mary, tells of her introduction to stepfamily reality. An accomplished child-and-adolescent therapist, this intelligent woman was certain that becoming a stepmother of four teenage sons was within her abilities. After all, she specialized in connecting with kids and understood their common teenage struggles and immature behavior. But she wasn't prepared for her own emotional reactions to these behaviors when they became a part of her life. After a wonderful wedding and weeklong honeymoon with her husband in Hawaii, Mary returned home to discover all four boys rollerblading inside the house on her hardwood floors. Welcome home and welcome to real life! As you can tell, they had a few things to work through before the family could experience a true honeymoon.

PRESS ON!

While on a recent flight to Chicago, the pilot of my (Ron's) airplane came on the loudspeaker to caution the passengers: "As you can tell, we're experiencing some turbulence," he said. "We've turned on the Fasten Seat Belt sign for your protection, and we want you to know that if you get out of your seat and break your arm, it's on your nickel." While the passengers didn't appreciate his tone, we did value the caution. Anyone trying to build a marriage in a stepfamily should heed these words of caution: "Buckle your seat belts and remain seated. The ride ahead may be bumpy for a while, but it will smooth out as you go. Press on, and don't jump out of the plane!"

COUPLE POSITIONING SYSTEM (CPS)

Where are you NOW? (Identify and Discuss Your Results)

a. Make a list of everyone in your "stepfamily forest." Be sure to include ex-spouses and members of the other households, i.e., anyone who has relational influence with you or your children (adult and minor children included).

b. Which relationships are difficult to manage? Which ones are assets to your marriage?

c. If married, share with each other how you think your marriage has changed since the wedding. How is life more complicated than you anticipated? How have stepfamily matters increased or decreased your couple satisfaction?

d. For those not yet married, what is your reaction to learning that couple satisfaction is more influenced by stepfamily matters after the wedding than it typically is before the wedding?

Where would you like to be? (Discuss Issues)

a. What strengths do you not possess right now? Don't try to resolve any issues yet, but envision how your relationship might look once this aspect is stronger.

b. In what ways do you feel overwhelmed when you think about what could be improved in your relationship?

How do you get there? (Develop Your Action Plan)

a. Continue to build on the strengths that you identified in chapter 2—keep doing the positive things you are doing well.

b. Develop your action plan: What might be a first step toward making your vision for a better relationship a reality? Decide what the first step for each of you might be and begin living it out very intentionally. Don't worry if it feels phony or contrived; just take the first step toward change and evaluate the results later.

c. Revisit your plan: In another week or so, set a time to review your progress.

d. What is your plan to get educated regarding stepfamily development?

Want to learn more about stepfamily living? In addition to this book, we highly recommend you read Ron's book *The Smart Stepfamily: Seven Steps to a Healthy Family* and check out the DVD series, available at *www.SuccessfulStepfamilies.com*.

Remember, the goal is to turn your stumbling blocks (issues) into stepping-stones (strengths).

Chapter 4

Positioning Yourself for Change

If you've ever been lost or worried about finding your way to an
unfamiliar destination, let us be your guide. We'll tell you how to get
wherever you want to go. No more fumbling with maps or hunting
for street signs. There's less wasted time and more peace of mind when
you use our global positioning system.

—What a GPS device might promise

NEVERLOST

I'll never forget the first time I (Ron) rented a car from Hertz with the NeverLost GPS direction system. Punch in the address of your destination and it plans your course and tells you which way to turn first. A calm and assuring voice even provides audio directions so you can keep your eye on the road. "Merge right one lane," it said as I approached the airport exit. "Exit number 31 approaching." And boy, it wasn't kidding. I topped a hill and it was time to exit! But thanks to NeverLost I was prepared.

After exiting the freeway, I spotted what I thought was the entrance to the airport rental car return. I ignored NeverLost and turned right, quickly realizing that I had taken a wrong turn. I pulled over to the side of the road and checked my GPS device, hoping it could right my wrong. To my amazement, it had already begun recalculating where I needed to go next to get me back on track.

In order to determine which way someone needs to go, Never-Lost always begins by calculating where you are now. At this point in the book you are probably getting a feel for what is going well in your relationship and how your marriage could grow. You are getting a more intimate portrait of where your relationship is now. But the analysis of your current couple position gained from the combined perspective of this book and your Couple Checkup Report are not yet complete. There's one more macro perspective of your relationship that we'd like to explore with you before beginning to help you enhance the specific elements of your marriage. It has to do with your Couple Type.

FIVE TYPES OF MARRIED COUPLES

Previous research by David and his colleagues at Life Innovations has identified five distinct types of marriage.[1] Each type has certain attributes, that is, a combination of strengths and weaknesses that are characteristic of those couples. When considered as a whole, these combined attributes describe the couple's relational style more fully than when we examined them individually. The Couple Types are summarized below.

Vitalized couples. Overall, this type of marriage represents the happiest couples and is reflected in the fact that they have the highest satisfaction scores on most aspects of their relationship and a low divorce rate compared to other couple types. One three-year longitudinal study found that 60 percent of vitalized couples were happily married.[2] Vitalized couples have many strengths, including conflict resolution, communication, and sexuality. Individuals in vitalized marriages rarely consider divorce (only 14 percent).[3]

Donna and Joe have been married for almost twenty years.

Five Types of Married Couples

Mean Positive Agreement (PCA)

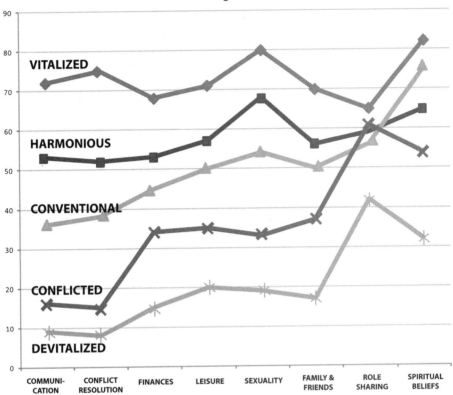

Each has a strong personality. In the past this led to conflict over parenting and stepparenting matters, but over the years they learned to respect each other for the unique contributions each makes to the marriage and parenting. Plus, hard work and determination has brought about healthy relationships with each other's children. With two of their combined five children, this process was stressful and slow (things didn't smooth out until the children were well into their adult years), but their perseverance finally paid off.

Donna and Joe display their commitment together by speaking well of each other in public. Each works hard on the job and strives to grow as an individual person—recognizing that qualities like love, patience, kindness, gentleness, and self-control improve every aspect

Vitalized Couple

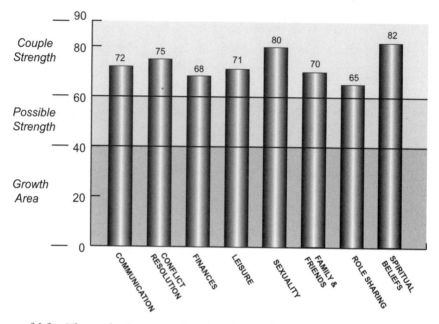

of life. Through the years Joe has learned to express humility in negotiating with Donna regarding her children, while Donna has worked to improve her willingness to make sacrifices for Joe's youngest child, who has boomeranged back to their home after college. A shared Christian value system has provided motivation to grow in these individual and collective ways, and it keeps them unified in how they spend their time, money, and energy. Life together has had many valleys, including the loss of a child in a tragic accident. But a strong commitment to their marriage has carried them through.

Harmonious couples. Like vitalized couples, many harmonious couples are very happy. They have many relationship strengths and possible strengths, but not as many as vitalized couples. Only 28 percent have ever considered divorce.[4] They are generally satisfied with many areas of their relationship including the roles each partner plays in the family (how they divide household responsibilities and tasks), sexuality, spiritual beliefs, and communication. Lower scores in the parenting domain (not shown in the chart) reflect the struggle to bring different parenting styles into cooperation and work together in leading the family.

Stan and Carrie make time for fun together each week. Sex is an important part of their relationship and often helps them to reconnect after a disagreement. They share chores around the house, work together fairly well in deciding how to spend their money, but struggle to manage their children together. Each is quite capable of interacting with Carrie's kids, but they don't agree on how to discipline. Carrie tries to compensate for Stan's temper and his high expectations of her kids. Stan is frustrated that she lets them "get away with so much," making him "pick up the slack." Another stress in their marriage is Carrie's ex-husband, whose jealous attitude and inconsistent parenting complicates the couple's parenting efforts. In spite of these challenges, Carrie and Stan consider each other best friends (they also have a few cute pet names for each other that their children love to repeat in public).

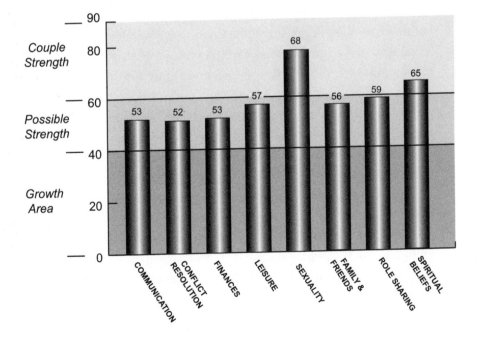

Harmonious Couple

Conventional Couple

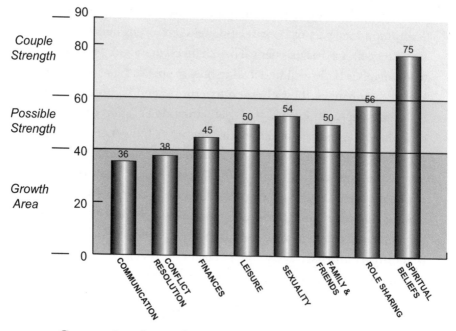

Conventional couples. These couples are moderately happy but have many weak aspects in their marriage. We refer to them as "conventional" because while they are not satisfied with certain aspects of their marriage, they are determined to stay together. The external dynamics of marriage (such as the task of raising children) as well as religious convictions keep these couples together despite only moderate happiness. The strengths of these couples include shared parenting (not shown here), strong connections with family and friends, division of roles, and the shared religious conviction of the home.

Conventional couples have lower scores on the more internal dynamics of marriage. They report dissatisfaction with the personality of their spouse (not shown on the graph here), and they have poor communication and conflict resolution skills. But despite the fact that more than half of these couples are not happy and over one-third (37 percent) of them have considered divorce, this couple type has the lowest rate of divorce.[5] They are committed to staying married no matter what.

Carlos and Juanita love their kids. Each brought two to the marriage after several years of single parenting (focused entirely on their children). Even after four years of marriage, Carlos and Juanita spend most of their non-working hours interacting with their children and supporting their activities and studies. This typically leads the couple (and family) in different directions as each concentrates on the activities of their own children. As it turns out, Juanita has decided this investment in her children keeps their marriage together because, as she explains, "since we don't communicate well, it's better that we fill our time with the kids rather than argue."

Carlos and Juanita attend church each week with their family and volunteer in the children's ministry, believing wholeheartedly that spirituality is the most important value in life and that giving back through service is important. Spiritual convictions keep them solidly stable in their marriage. They have many shared friends and frequently surround themselves with extended family or attend social functions. From the outside, this marriage looks better than it really is. They are roommates with a common cause: children and church.

Conflicted couples. Unfortunately these couples are unhappy most of the time. With numerous growth areas and few relationship strengths, it's not surprising that a majority of individuals in these marriages have considered divorce (73 percent). Indeed, in one three-year longitudinal study, 53 percent did divorce.[6] They are called "conflicted" since they disagree on many topics and have low scores on many aspects of their marriage. Conflicted couples commonly seek marital therapy (or should consider doing so).

Stephanie and Jim are passionate people. A quick courtship and wedding following Stephanie's painful divorce and the death of Jim's first wife seemed to resolve their sadness. However, when their infatuation waned, their passion shifted to trying to change each other. Now they argue about many things. They find themselves at odds, whether the issue be money, sex, each other's children, or the ex-mothers-in-law. Stephanie complains to her girlfriends about how Jim reminds her of her ex (something she never noticed before the wedding) and

Conflicted Couple

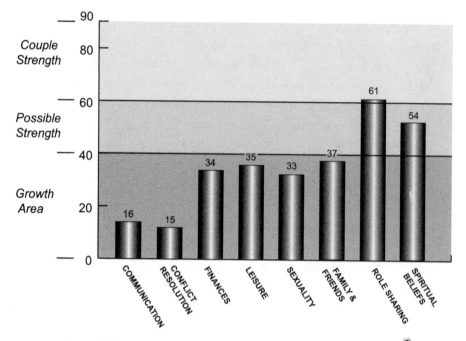

wonders if she married him too quickly. Jim never questions whether she loves him but knows he doesn't have her respect. Feeling like a failure as a husband only pushes him to spend more time at work, where he knows he is competent. This, of course, leaves Stephanie to spend extra time with his teenage children, of whom she disapproves most of the time. Jim's kids complain that they now have greater restrictions because Stephanie parents them like she does her younger children. When all else fails, Stephanie and Jim hold on to the memory of happier days and hope that will see them through.

Devitalized couples. These couples are extremely unhappy. They need to improve nearly every aspect of their relationships. Most of them have considered divorce (90 percent) and in two-thirds of the couples (69 percent) both spouses are dissatisfied.[7] These couples (along with conflicted couples) frequently seek out marital therapy or couple enrichment programs.

Devitalized Couple

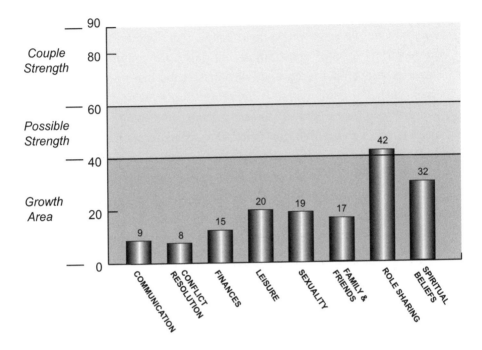

David and Laura feel very defeated most of the time and often shield themselves from the negativity of the other. They've learned that avoiding each other is the lesser evil among many, even though it means functioning separately as parents and feeling isolated as partners. There is a great deal of stress in their relationship, and they often speak to each other with sarcasm, accusation, and criticism which, of course, ignites defensiveness, hurt, and anger. For example, when Laura asks David's son, Caleb, to finish his kitchen chores, David defends Caleb and makes excuses for his behavior. This infuriates Laura's oldest child, who finds it unfair that Caleb isn't required to do what she is expected to do. In arguments, Laura has begun to talk about the possibility of divorce, even though that's not what she wants. At this point, it just seems to be the only way to find relief.

POSITIONING YOURSELF FOR CHANGE

How does understanding couple types help your relationship? First, it gives perspective. As these couple types demonstrate, there are a variety of marriages. Not all marriages are comprised of the same relationship strength-and-weakness combinations. Knowing your particular combination is important to discovering where you are now and how to grow your relationship. For example, harmonious couples can build on their moderate strengths such as spiritual beliefs and affection/sexuality, whereas conventional couples need mostly to improve their communication patterns and problem-solving strategies. Vitalized couples should celebrate their strengths and affirm each other, but they should be careful not to take the future—or each other—for granted. Conflicted and devitalized couples need to honestly face the deficits in their relationships. They may have been blind to them in the past, but it's time to acknowledge them and face them head-on. We can only pretend at relationships for a season; conflicted and devitalized couples should find a local marriage education program or therapist soon.

If you haven't done so already, look at your Couple Checkup Report to discover what type of couple your relationship most closely resembles. Look at the pattern of strengths and weaknesses in your relationship and consider the overall nature of your relationship right now. Affirm what is going well and consider what isn't. This can immediately give you ideas about what you might want to change in your relationship. Remember, at this point, you're only trying to discover what needs to change. *How* to change will come later as we examine relationship dimensions more closely.

Second, understanding the different types of marriage can help you to identify what type of marriage you ultimately want. Couples should not assume that their partner wants a vitalized relationship; given the painful pasts that many people in remarriage have experienced, we have learned that not everyone is willing to take the emotional risks required to build a vitalized marriage. We realize this is counterintuitive. "Doesn't everyone want a great marriage?" you might ask. The answer is yes, until building a great marriage requires more of them than they are comfortable giving.

Be sure to honestly assess your goals for your marriage and then check out your partner's goals. This too can help you "recalculate" what needs to happen in order for your marriage to reach its stated destination.

Finally, if discovering your couple type has brought discouragement, remember that you can change! Your couple type is where you are today; tomorrow can be different.

FOCUS ON YOUR STRENGTHS

Whether you have been together for a few months or for many years, one purpose of this book is to get you to focus more on your couple strengths than on the dissatisfying aspects of your marriage. We have found that how much a couple focuses on strengths versus problems changes over time. In the earlier stages of a relationship, people naturally think about and notice the things they like about their partner, overlooking or regarding as unimportant more negative qualities. This is the "love is blind" phenomenon. Of course, the blinders tend to come off after couples have been together for a while. At that point we commonly see married couples doing the opposite—focusing on the negative aspects of their partner and their relationship, and not thinking as much about their couple strengths.

Focus is power. What you focus on will tend to gain importance and influence your perceptions. As a child, you may have experienced this phenomenon with a magnifying glass and the sun. Even though the sun is 93 million miles away, by focusing its energy in one area, you can create enough heat to make a fire.

Focus impacts your couple relationship. If you focus on the positive, you will naturally become more aware of the positive and enable your relationship to grow and thrive. If you focus on the negative, you will feel greater discouragement and forecast a negative future. We are not advocating ignoring unhealthy or destructive patterns of relating; you certainly must diminish these components of marriage, and conflicted and devitalized couples will need to work actively to do so. We are simply inviting you to adjust your attention toward what is going right in your marriage rather than focusing exclusively on what is not. Then, and only then, can you build a more vital and mutually satisfying relationship.

COUPLE POSITIONING SYSTEM (CPS)

Where are you NOW? (Identify and Discuss Your Results)

a. Review your Couple Checkup Report to see what Couple Type you are most similar to. The chart below summarizes the strengths and key growth dimensions of each type.

b. The Couple Scores in the Summary of Strength and Growth Areas graph describe how much you agree with each other in a positive way about important aspects of your relationship.

Five Types of Married Couples		
Couple Type	Strengths	Key Growth Dimensions / Cautions
1. Vitalized	• Many very high scores. • Very high couple agreement and happiness with most aspects of their marriage. • Strong "internal" dynamics (e.g., communication, financial management, and shared spirituality). • Strong "external" dynamics (e.g., family, friends, and relationship roles).	• Not slipping into complacency. • Not taking each other for granted.
2. Harmonious	• Many high scores. • High couple agreement and happiness with many aspects of the marriage. • Strong "internal dynamics" related to shared leisure time, communication, and sexuality.	• High scores provide a solid base from which to grow, but you need to be proactive. • Parenting (not shown in the graphs, but included in your Checkup Report) likely needs improved cooperation, agreement, and follow-through. In stepfamilies, stress in parenting can be detrimental to your marriage.

3. Conventional	• Moderate scores across most areas. • Strong aspects include role definitions and spiritual convictions.	• Critical "internal" skills like communication and conflict resolution need attention. • Emotional closeness and intimacy may be lacking. • Give more attention to the couple relationship and a little less to children, friends, and extended family.
4. Conflicted	• Strongest areas are roles and spirituality.	• Because "internal" skills like communication and conflict resolution are lacking, cooperation, closeness, and handling clashes in personality will be difficult. Attention must be given to key areas like communication and conflict.
5. Devitalized	• Mainly growth areas. • Few couple strengths exist. • Any existing moderate strengths should be improved first.	• Focus on any positive behaviors of your partner and praise them. • Take time to talk and try to resolve current issues. • If no improvement, seek marital therapy. • Couple therapy intensives can be found at *www.Successful Stepfamilies.com.*

Where would you like to be? (Discuss Issues)

a. What are your first reactions to your Couple Type? (Remember, this is a snapshot of your relationship now, but you have the opportunity to improve the number of strengths you have by working on the growth areas.)

b. What concerns do you have? What affirmation do you feel?

c. If you have a vitalized, harmonious, or conventional Couple Type, share which moderate strength area you would like to intentionally try to improve.

d. If you have a conflicted or devitalized Couple Type, seriously consider one or two growth areas of your relationship that need attention. Be sure to affirm the moderate strengths you do have. Read the corresponding chapter in this book so you can build on what is going pretty well at this point in time.

e. Discuss what your ideal Couple Type will look like. Keep in mind that a vitalized relationship will require effort by both partners.

How do you get there? (Develop Your Action Plan)

a. Be sure to continue behaviors that contribute to your strengths. For example, harmonious couples will want to continue their good communication skills; conventional couples will want to build on their shared spiritual values. What actions will you continue?

b. Begin a list of behaviors that might need to change for your relationship to improve over time. Try not to be defensive with each other as you share these items. List behaviors that need to decrease (e.g., defensiveness, critical and angry talk, being child-focused to the detriment of your marriage) and the behaviors you'd like to see more of (e.g., random acts of kindness, expressing appreciation for each other, playing together, etc.).

c. Renew your commitment to continue reading this book and working on improving your relationship (or participating in your study group). Remember, now that you have an honest, objective understanding of your relationship, you are positioned for change.

Chapter 5

Mapping Closeness and Flexibility

In your couple relationship, you either repeat what you learned in your family or you tend to do the opposite.

—David H. Olson

Every couple has a relational culture. The culture—or style—shifts with the passage of time and the coming and going of children. Two key elements of this relationship style can be described as *closeness* and *flexibility*. For example, newly married couples without children are free to spend extra time with each other whenever they want (flexibility), and often say things like, "I just don't know if I could live without you" (closeness). Those of us who have been married a while know, of course, that we *can* live without each other and *will* once the children arrive!

The Checkup Report includes a Couple Map (a Family Map is also included in reports for premarital couples), which is a very sophisticated instrument that assesses the level of closeness and flexibility in your relationship. Part of the Couple Positioning System, it helps you to distinguish your current relational style from twenty-five possible styles (i.e., where you are now), and it allows you to share with your partner how you would prefer your relational style to be (where you want to go). It also links you to your past by assessing the style of the family in which you grew up. This is important to know because each of us tends to gravitate toward either reproducing that style in our own marriage and family or away from it. It serves as a magnet, either pulling you closer or pushing you further from the relational style of your childhood family.

If at this point you have not chosen to take the online Checkup, you can complete the quiz at the end of the chapter to plot how you perceive your relationship on the Couple Map. The Couple Map will help you estimate and visually depict the nature of your relationship. If you have taken the Couple Checkup, you will be able to simply turn to that portion of the report (premarital couples will also have a Family Map).

COUPLE AND FAMILY CLOSENESS

Closeness refers to the level of emotional bonding in your relationship. It involves the feelings of closeness or connectedness, the action you take to be involved with each other, as well as how you balance time together and time apart, i.e., your intimate connection time and your private time. As indicated on the Couple and Family Map, the intersection of these aspects of closeness results in either a balanced or unbalanced relationship. As you will see later, when combined with the flexibility scale, a third type of relationship is created: mid-range.

The word *closeness* is generally associated with *feeling* close to one's partner. Our study certainly found that to be the case with strong couples. But closeness also involves *doing* things together that facilitate the feelings of closeness. In fact, our study revealed that the contrast between happy and unhappy couples is best measured by the things couples do to create warmth and affection for each other in the relationship. At least 94 percent of satisfied couples have hobbies and interests that bring them together, and they find it easy

Couple and Family Map

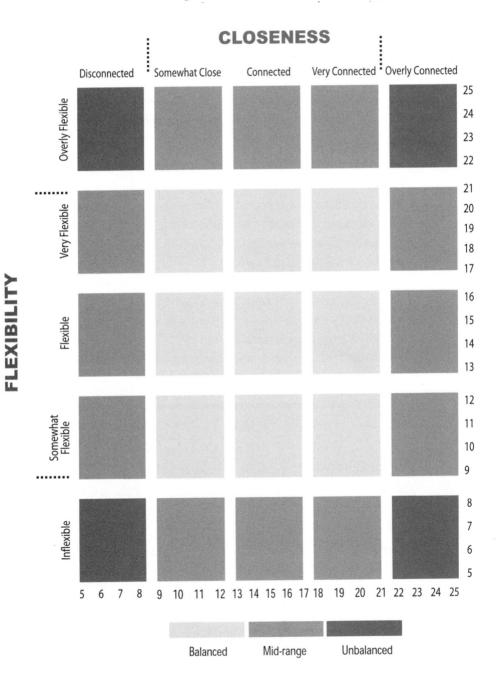

to think of things to do together (compared to 62 percent or less of discouraged couples). In addition, a full 94 percent said togetherness was a top priority for them, revealing strong couples' intentional effort to invest in their relationship. *Doing* things that facilitate closeness certainly contributes to *feeling* close.

=============== **Getting Close:** ===============
The *doing* and *feeling* of closeness

Vibrant Couples:
- Feel confidence and trust in each other and feel secure with each other.
- Include each other in important decisions.
- Share leadership within their relationship.
- Have a mutual respect for each other.
- Have similar likes and interests.
- Are committed to spending time together on a regular basis and intentionally plan ways to be together.
- Feel the freedom to ask each other for help.
- Choose to be loyal to each other.
- Balance time with family and friends so as not to take away from their relationship.

Closeness also involves balance. Every healthy relationship has a balance of time spent together and time apart. Couples have both a desire to be together (spending time together is a priority) and a respect for the individual interests, pursuits, and freedoms of their partner. In strong relationships, individuals place emphasis on the "self" as well as the "we."

They strive for an appropriate amount of sharing, loyalty, intimacy, and independence. This dance of intimacy is not easily achieved. It demands attention and good communication since couples naturally have times in their relationship when they spend more time together and generate many close feelings, and other seasons of the relationship that demand more personal space. Taken together, these natural

Five Levels of Closeness

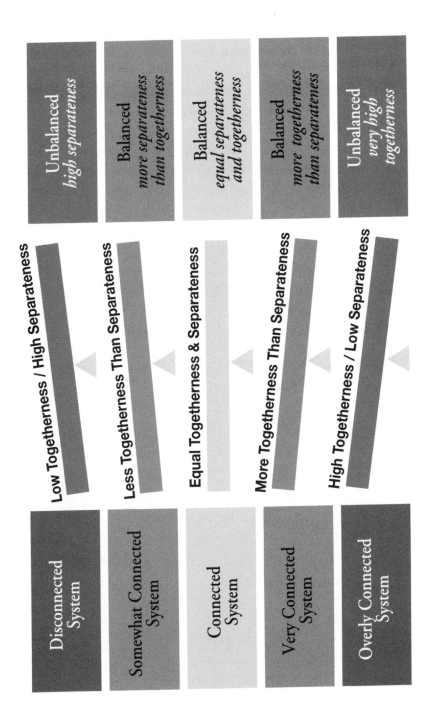

Unbalanced
high separateness

Balanced
*more separateness
than togetherness*

Balanced
*equal separateness
and togetherness*

Balanced
*more togetherness
than separateness*

Unbalanced
*very high
togetherness*

Low Togetherness / High Separateness

Less Togetherness Than Separateness

Equal Togetherness & Separateness

More Togetherness Than Separateness

High Togetherness / Low Separateness

Disconnected
System

Somewhat Connected
System

Connected
System

Very Connected
System

Overly Connected
System

rhythms of marriage combine to create a "balanced" relationship, but couples should always guard against spending too much time at either extreme.

Over time, unbalanced relationships overemphasize either the distance in the relationship (disconnected) or the need for closeness and mutual dependency (overly connected). It is these extremes that couples need to guard against. Each extreme has an emotionally debilitating impact on relationships. Too much distance and one or both partners feel excluded, vulnerable, expendable, or lonely. Too much closeness and someone (or both) feels smothered, disrespected, or controlled.

Matt has a very high need for closeness. His father and mother divorced when he was very young, so he grew up without a great deal of family stability. He mainly lived with his mother and felt to blame that his father wasn't around much. His grandfather served as a surrogate father for a few years, but he died an untimely death when Matt was just ten years old. Because closeness in his childhood family relationships was not something he experienced (disconnected), he longed for it in his adult romantic relationships.

Matt's wife, Sherry, grew up in a hardworking middle-class family. While they loved one another deeply, the demands of earning a living kept parents and children going in multiple directions. As a result, Sherry learned quickly how to remain emotionally and financially independent from loved ones. She prided herself on working her way through technical school after having a child in high school. A later marriage added a child, but the marriage ended in divorce. This series of fragmented romantic relationships only fueled her emotional independence as a parent and adult.

When Matt and Sherry met, they quickly became romantically and sexually involved. Matt was enthralled with the amount of attention he received from Sherry. She seemed to be a dedicated mom but still went out of her way to make time for him. Sherry saw in Matt the kind of stability she wanted her children to experience (something she didn't have as a child), so she pursued him with passion. Her physical and sexual availability and his need for closeness locked together and blinded Matt to the temporary nature of their emotional relationship.

While dating, the couple was overly connected (unbalanced). After a rushed courtship and wedding, Sherry didn't feel the need to pursue Matt as much as before. A significant drop in connectedness and time together produced a great deal of anxiety in Matt. He complained to a friend, "Now that we're married, Sherry is much more worried about being a mom than she is a wife."

Neither Matt nor Sherry is to blame for what is happening. Yet each is responsible. Together they need to:

- Understand their family of origin style so they know what is familiar and why it draws them toward a similar or different style in their couple relationship.
- Become aware of their own and the other's desires for closeness so they can choose to serve each other's needs.
- Discuss how they can work toward the healthy balanced dimensions of closeness.
- Talk about how they can be in tune with the other's preferred level of closeness.

You will have an opportunity to evaluate the closeness in your relationship at the end of this chapter.

COUPLE AND FAMILY FLEXIBILITY

"A high station in life is earned by the gallantry with which appalling experiences are survived with grace."

Tennessee Williams

"Do you wish to be great? Then begin by being. Do you desire to construct a vast and lofty fabric? Think first about the foundations of humility. The higher your structure is to be, the deeper must be its foundation."

Saint Augustine

The world has seen a plethora of marriage books. Bookstores are filled with rows of books that address the commonly understood aspects of healthy relationships: communication, resolving conflict, managing money, a healthy sexual relationship, etc. Marriage books have a lot in common. But when was the last time you read a marriage book that encouraged you to be flexible? Likely never. Until now.

Our research discovered that a healthy dose of flexibility in the couple's relationship and individual attitudes toward the management of their family was one of the top five predictors of a satisfying relationship (number five to be exact), and accounted for nearly 20 percent of what predicted a healthy, strong remarriage relationship. But what is *flexibility*? Kay knows.

Five years into her remarriage, Kay discovered just how life-sustaining and conflict-reducing having a flexible attitude was. Surrounded by four children (two of hers and two of his), she and her husband dealt continuously with the hectic schedules, between-home conflicts, and parenting dilemmas that most stepfamilies face. When asked how she was able to cope with the stresses and pressures that were out of her control, Kay replied, "I've learned how to let go. I learned early on, for example, that letting the other home have the kids on Christmas Day was not only a gift to them, but to myself. I really wanted the kids with us on that special day, but I realized that giving my children and my ex that time helped everyone enjoy the holidays more. Besides, I found that Christmas alone with my husband was not a bad thing. In fact, it was a marriage-building thing. Often I find myself giving in, not because it's my turn, but because it creates peace for my children—and that is more important than fairness. Besides, in time, I have seen this giving attitude returned to us by the other home."

What Kay discovered is that flexibility—the quality of being adaptable—allowed her to find a bearable solution to the natural desire of both her and her ex-husband to spend Christmas Day with their children. Not only did a flexible attitude help her find her way around this seeming impasse, it empowered her to find a blessing or two along the way.

FINDING BALANCE IN FLEXIBILITY

Should Kay always take the backseat when dealing with her ex-husband? Absolutely not. Flexibility must be tempered with stability and consistency. Finding the balance is important.

Flexibility refers to how open to change a couple's relationship is in the areas of leadership, relationship boundaries, roles within the marriage, and problem solving. Healthy couple relationships maintain a balance between a predictable pattern of interaction ("stability") and the ability to adapt or change when circumstances call for it ("flexibility").

Olympic ice-skating duos are amazing to watch. With tremendous fluidity and seemingly effortless grace, the man and woman dance on the ice while performing difficult maneuvers that require careful coordination. While they make it appear easy, two difficult actions are at work: flexibility and stability. Flexibility is required to bend, spin, turn, or move in sequenced motion, while stability allows them to share the weight of each maneuver, brace when returning to the ice after an aerial wonder, and support each other's movement on the ice. Marriage requires this same delicate dance.

When it comes to financial management and commitment to the relationship, for example, a husband and wife need to know that they can expect stability and consistency from each other. This gives the marriage a sense of security because each knows what to expect from the other. On the other hand, couples need the capacity to change as life demands. As children grow and enter new phases of life, parenting responses must change. Without flexibility, parents try to manage their teenagers the same way they did when the children were in preschool. Making a child's decisions regarding bedtime, mealtime, and playtime was fine when the child was four; doing so when the child is fifteen is sure to bring conflict within the home. Therefore, both stability and flexibility are important to the couple relationship over time.

Five Levels of Flexibility

Overly Flexible System	Very Flexible System	Flexible System	Somewhat Flexible System	Inflexible System
High Change / Low Stability	More Change Than Stability	Equal Change & Stability	Less Change Than Stability	Low Change / High Stability
Unbalanced *a lot of change*	Balanced *considerable change*	Balanced *moderate change*	Balanced *some change*	Unbalanced *very little change*

Couple Flexibility: Making Life Work	
Happy Couples	Unhappy Couples
Are creative in how they handle differences (80%) and are open to exploring new solutions with each other.	Have a rigid mentality to problem solving and get stuck. (72%)
Compromise and seek win-win solutions; they consider the other's opinions and are open to being influenced by the other. (96%)	Seek to personally win and may fear giving the other too much control. (48%)
Work together to organize their daily life, schedule, and household. (84%)	Cannot seem to get organized. (61%)
Work as a team to make decisions; they seek unity in leading their household. (96%)	Make most decisions independently of the other. (41%)
Are humble and willing to change when necessary. (94%)	Find change difficult or only one person is willing to adapt as needed. (44%)

RELATIONAL FLEXIBILITY

Our research uncovered three key dimensions of relational flexibility: how couples handle differences, couple organization and leadership, and a willingness to take life as it comes. Together these qualities contribute significantly to a satisfying marriage relationship. Let's consider each.

Handling differences. When it comes to handling differences in the relationship, unhappy couples tend to get stuck in a rut. For example, every couple experiences conflicts due to differences in preference. In fact, research has suggested that happy and unhappy couples alike share the same number of conflicts.[1] Unhappy couples just can't get through the differences—they get stuck in them. Healthy couples, by comparison, are much more likely to find creative solutions to their differences and work them out (80 percent versus only

28 percent of unsatisfied couples). They are able to think outside the box (or outside their own conceptualization of what the solution should be) and are open to explore different ideas.

Healthy couples also demonstrate flexibility through compromise. A full 96 percent of vitalized couples—twice as many as unhappy couples—find the win-win solution when it comes to disagreements (which usually means both partners must bend a little). They are open to being influenced by the other, which stands in stark contrast to unhappy couples, who fight "to win" in disagreements. But why take this stand? We wonder if part of the reason some couples find compromise difficult is because they fear giving over control to the other.

Rhonda had two children out of wedlock; for ten years she was their sole provider and emotional nurturer. When she married Reggie, she had no idea how difficult it would be to release some of that responsibility to her husband. Letting go of her control so he could be a role model in their lives was what Rhonda dreamed of during courtship, but after the wedding, it scared her to death. She found herself vetoing his parenting suggestions and discounting his input in decisions. Reggie felt pushed further and further to the outside of the family's experience, and his resentment grew steadily. It was only after Rhonda challenged herself to make room for Reggie's influence that they were able to work out an agreeable parenting system that benefited the children and facilitated their closeness.

Getting organized. Healthy flexibility is always balanced with stability. This is especially true when it comes to the leadership of the home. Being able to adapt to life's circumstances does not mean an erratic, chaotic home environment. Happy couples are much more likely to feel organized in life than unsatisfied couples (61 percent of whom feel disorganized). Not only that, but the way they get organized is different, too.

A much higher percentage of satisfied couples (by a margin of 37 percent) share decision making. They work as a team to manage their home and life, while unsatisfied couples take a more independent approach to decisions. Again, we suspect that trust issues may lie at the heart of this disconnected approach to the relationship. To avoid further hurt or rejection, partners may be tempted to maintain more independence, which, of course, only reinforces emotional distance in the marriage. For many then, becoming more flexible in their relationship equals an increase in emotional risk. If you find yourself struggling with this fear, remember that without relational risk, there can be no relational gain.

Taking life as it comes. A stepfamily is no place for a rigid person. By nature, because of their complexity, remarried families require multiple changes throughout life. Inflexible people—who have rigid ideas of how family life should be—find themselves feeling worn out by the never-ending changes that result when multiple households, parents, and differing levels of bondedness with children collide. For example, stepmothers often report that they had no idea how difficult it would be to have their husband's ex-wife have so much influence over their family's schedule. "Just when I think I know what our weekend is going to be like, he gets a phone call from his ex and everything changes. I wish I had more control over my own life." That is a very familiar feeling for many remarried couples. Yet, since multiple-household families have multiple forces of influence, the ability to adapt—to take life as it comes—becomes a point of survival for many. With multiple forces of influence, people with rigid approaches to life find themselves constantly battling what they cannot control. But a flexible person is able to adapt, bend as needed, and get through the change. Even better is when *both partners* can adjust to change.

Our study found that in 94 percent of happy couples both partners showed a willingness to change (compared to just 44 percent of unsatisfied couples). Managing change is a couple's matter, not just the task of one of the partners. When both adapt, the net result for the couple is a sense of unity as together they move around the forces of life.

AT THE HEART OF FLEXIBILITY

So what makes someone flexible? How do you teach someone to be flexible? When our research uncovered the importance of flexibility, these questions began to trouble us. Is flexibility a natural personality trait that people either possess or don't? What attitudes are at the heart of a flexible lifestyle?

One key attitude is *humility*. The unpretentious person who is not prideful or self-seeking, but able to surrender themselves in loving service to their mate, will find making adjustments (flexibility) in life much easier. They are not a doormat or codependent as some fear; rather, they are open to the influence of their partner and able to learn what is pleasing to them. Instead of maintaining a wall of pride when a complaint is offered, they calmly receive it and consider its merits. Self-change follows when necessary.

Humility also shares power in a relationship, rather than posturing for it. This leads to the joint decision making of healthy couples and the ability to compromise that we found in our research. And when both persons demonstrate a humble servant's heart in the marriage, a competition is created, but not one that most people fear. Instead of a competition for power or control, humble couples create a competition for kindness. This environment mutually feeds and cares for each person as they build each other up in the marriage.

A second relational attitude that feeds couple flexibility is *grace*. Most people recognize that in spiritual terms, grace, broadly defined, refers to any good thing that comes from God. Expressed in marriage, the graceful person seeks to bring good things to the life of their partner (and extended family). They seek the good of the other and try to nurture the well-being of their mate.

But perhaps more important, a person filled with grace offers forgiveness—even when undeserved. They seek to reconcile the relationship when a conflict or barrier exists, which leads to giving second chances and creative problem solving. Of course, forgiveness is emotionally much easier to grant when the other is humbly accepting responsibility for how they have hurt you, but forgiveness should not be offered only when the other "deserves it." At times, it is simply a free gift.

Lisa married Jacob, the father of two teenage children, about three years after his first wife's death to cancer. Obviously the children had strong emotional ties to their mother and struggled to accept their dad's remarriage and the presence of a stepmother despite their generally amicable relationship with Lisa. "It just feels like Mom is dying all over again," his fourteen-year-old son explained. But the children's resistance wasn't all that Lisa and Jacob were dealing with. His deceased wife's parents remained very close to their grandchildren, and they too found it difficult to adapt to anyone who would "try to take their daughter's place."

Time and time again, Lisa found herself isolated as an emotional outsider, especially when her husband appropriately ministered to his children's sadness. And yet a grace-filled heart led her to return good gifts to her stepchildren and in-laws. She reminded herself that their sadness was not a personal affront to her, but an appropriate response to their loss. She acknowledged that she would never hold first place in their lives—and didn't need to in order to have a respectful, likable relationship. Even though her heart was open to deepening her bonds with them, she knew she had to give them the gift of time as they worked through their grief. Similarly, her humility empowered her ability to serve her husband, even when he found himself consumed by the sadness of his family. Eventually, over time, grief found its place in the home, not as a barrier to new relationships, but as an expression of honor for the past, and Lisa and Jacob's marriage matured. Her relationship with her stepchildren also continues to deepen.

Together, humility and grace form the foundations of couple flexibility. They reshape the heart of each individual away from selfishness and toward mutual consideration, surrender, and trust—qualities of every great, intimate marriage.

THE INTERSECTION OF CLOSENESS AND FLEXIBILITY

Closeness and flexibility can stand alone as separate relational concepts. But when we combine them on the Couple and Family Map, we see an intersection of these two powerful dimensions. Together they create a relational culture or style that either supports your relationship or works against it. (Look again at the Map on page 65 or at your results in the Couple Report.)

When the closeness and flexibility scores are in the balanced ranges, the couple's relational style is also balanced. Think of this as a green light at a traffic intersection—you have the go-ahead. If, however, one dimension is out of balance and the other is fine, the couple score becomes mid-range. Think of this as a yellow light. Caution is recommended. If both closeness and flexibility are out of balance, the couple composite score will be unbalanced. This is a serious red light, and attention needs to be given to balancing both dimensions of the relationship.

Let's consider an example. Research shows that it is quite common for couples to fall in the balanced region of Somewhat Close and Very Flexible during the adolescent years of parenting. This time of life requires a great deal of flexibility as teens try on new levels of independence. Parenting rules, for example, that worked well throughout the elementary years must be modified to allow for the teen's growth and maturation (flexibility). Given the increased demands of parenting during this phase of life, couples commonly report lower but still "somewhat close" levels of closeness. This is quite understandable during this season of life, and this couple style is still in the balanced regions. In addition, this style actually functions to support the demands of the marriage and family.

However, what if one parent in this home maintained a very inflexible style of parenting while the other tried to counterbalance with an overly flexible style? Parents with these extreme styles would frequently find themselves disagreeing about the children and would likely feel undercut by each other. Conflict would erupt on a regular basis. The impact on the couple closeness scale would likely be movement toward Disconnected. Such a relational style would not support the family at this season of life and would be detrimental to the marriage.

At the end of this chapter you will have the opportunity to consider how the intersection of your scores (your couple style) is either facilitating or hindering your family at this point in time. Plus, we will return to the Couple and Family Map in chapter 7 when we consider the most effective parenting styles for parents and stepparents.

YOUR FAMILY MAP

Dating and engaged couples taking the online Couple Checkup also receive a Family Map profile. Your family of origin—that is, the family you grew up in—still has a powerful influence in your life. The earlier story of Matt and Sherry demonstrates how Matt's sensitivity to Sherry's distance is connected to being rejected by his father as a child. Sherry's pride in remaining emotionally and financially independent is a consequence of her hardworking family of origin. Most people grossly underestimate how influential their family of origin is in who they are and the choices they make in relationships as an adult. This is especially true when stress or anxieties increase. We tend to revert to the scripts we learned and followed in our upbringing.

The Family Map page of your Couple Report provides feedback on the relational styles of your family of origin. This will help you gain a deeper understanding of yourself and your partner. Be sure to consider how this style has impacted your life, and share examples with your partner so he or she can come to more fully understand this dynamic in your life.

COUPLE POSITIONING SYSTEM (CPS)

Mapping Your Relationship

(Turn to the Couple Map of your report)

Where are you NOW? (Identify and Discuss Your Results)

a. Premarital couples only: Review your Family Map Results.

- Consider your family of origin relationship style. Can you share a story with your partner that helps him or her understand the report results?

- What part of your family would you like to re-create in this current family? What is similar or different already?

b. All couples: Review the Couple Map Results (or if you haven't take the online Checkup, complete the Couple Exercise on the following pages to determine where you are on the Couple Map).

- This is how you view the relationship now. Is it what you wish it to be? Why or why not?

- Become aware of each other's desires for closeness so you can choose to be responsive to your partner's needs for more or less connection and more or less flexibility.

- Stepparents: Be sure to consider your spouse's style with his or her children and how it compares to what you prefer or experienced as a child. How are these dynamics similar or different?

c. Discuss your Score Placement: The central white regions indicate balance; the four corners represent extreme scores in both closeness and flexibility ("unbalanced").

- What is the intersection of your results (flexibility and closeness)? How does this help or hinder your family at this season of life?

- If your score falls in an unbalanced region, discuss how you can work toward the healthier center regions. What needs to change?

- If your score is in the balanced regions, what should you continue to do? What slight modifications might you make?

Where would you like to be? (Discuss Issues)

a. In a perfect world, where would you prefer to be on the map? Point to a square that represents what you desire (take turns).

b. What makes this appealing to you?

c. Share how you each feel about the other's preference.

How do you get there? (Develop Your Action Plan)

a. Brainstorm a few things you could do to move toward your preferences.

b. Agree on one solution you will try.

c. Decide what you will each do to make the plan work.

d. Review the progress in one week.

COUPLE EXERCISE
(Only for couples who have not
taken the Couple Checkup)

Couple Closeness

1. How often do you spend free time together?

1	2	3	4	5
Never	Seldom	Sometimes	Often	Very Often

2. How committed are you to your partner?

1	2	3	4	5
Slightly	Somewhat	Generally	Very	Extremely

3. How close do you feel to your partner?

1	2	3	4	5
Not very close	Somewhat close	Generally close	Very close	Extremely close

4. How do you and your partner balance separateness and togetherness?

1	2	3	4	5
Mainly separateness	More separateness than togetherness	Equal togetherness and separateness	More togetherness than separateness	Mainly togetherness

5. How independent of or dependent on each other are you and your partner?

1	2	3	4	5
Very independent	More independent than dependent	Equally dependent and independent	More dependent than independent	Very dependent

Add your responses to these questions to get a total closeness score.

Couple Flexibility

1. What kind of leadership is there in your couple relationship?

1	2	3	4	5
One person usually leads	Leadership is sometimes shared	Leadership is generally shared	Leadership is usually shared	Leadership is unclear

2. How often do you and your partner do the same things (roles) around the house?

1	2	3	4	5
Almost always	Usually	Often	Sometimes	Seldom

3. What are the rules (written or unwritten) like in your relationship?

1	2	3	4	5
Rules very clear and very stable	Rules clear and generally stable	Rules clear and structured	Rules clear and flexible	Rules unclear and changing

4. How are decisions handled?

1	2	3	4	5
One person usually decides	Decisions are sometimes shared	Decisions are often shared	Decisions are usually shared	Decisions are rarely made

5. How much change occurs in your couple relationship?

1	2	3	4	5
Very little change	Little change	Some change	Considerable change	A great deal of change

Add your responses to these questions to get a total flexibility score.

Couple Map

1. Complete the Couple Map for how your relationship is now. You can also complete the exercise again to describe how you would ideally like your couple relationship to be.
2. Score the exercise for both the Now and the Ideal. Then plot both scores on the Couple and Family Map (See page 85).

		Closeness	Flexibility
Partner 1	Now	_____	_____
	Ideal	_____	_____
Partner 2	Now	_____	_____
	Ideal	_____	_____

3. Compare how you each described your relationship now on the Couple and Family Map. Discuss similarities and differences on couple closeness and couple flexibility.
4. Compare how you each described how you would ideally like your relationship to be. Discuss similarities and differences.
5. Discuss how you can work together to make your relationship more like what you each ideally would like.

Couple and Family Map

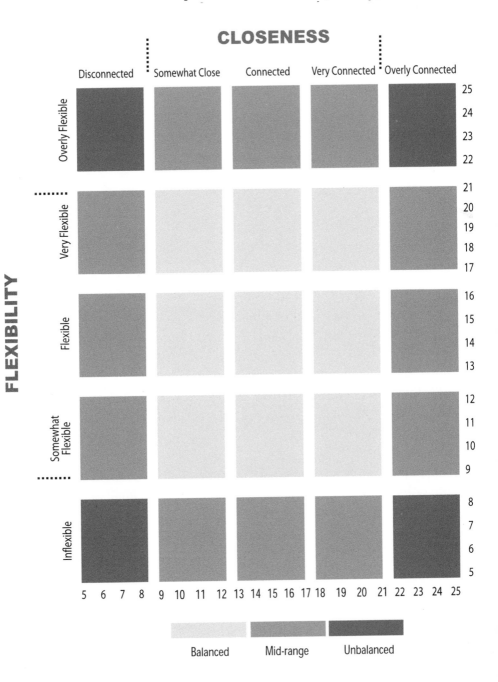

Chapter 6

Eyes Wide Open:
Finding Realistic Expectations

Before you marry keep both eyes open; after marriage shut one.
—Jamaican proverb

As long as I'm paying the bills, I expect authority over your kids.
—Stepfather of three

From my perspective, I would like to see my children have a mother again and our home have that center a wife brings. I really think I can accept her children and I think my children would not resent new stepsiblings.
—Father of four
Dating a woman with six children

Now that you've got the big picture regarding remarriage and your relationship in particular, let's begin to examine the most important aspects of successful relationships according to our study.

Imagine that you've just hopped into your rental car, entered your destination address into the GPS unit, and the display has calculated your driving path. As you put the car in drive, you close your eyes and press down on the accelerator. What do you think is about to happen? Or instead, what if you kept your eyes partly open but were so afraid of the road that you refused to press the accelerator? Bottom line: Neither approach is going to get you safely to your destination. The first will result in an accident, and the second in not moving at all.

Essentially the same dynamic is at play when couples close their eyes to their relationship or in fear refuse to move forward. Your Couple Report (Couple Positioning System) is telling you where you are and where you need to go to reach your destination. But if you don't open your eyes and engage the road, your expectations of what is to come and how to maneuver it will be far from realistic. In fact, your expectations will be detrimental to the journey. Likewise, if your fears of the future restrain the amount of self you are willing to give to the relationship, you'll never find the accelerator. You—and your relationship—will just sit in park.

EXPECTATIONS: THE IDEAL AND THE REAL

The Jamaican proverb quoted at the beginning of this chapter has it correct when it advises couples to keep both eyes open before marriage and one eye shut after the wedding. Unfortunately, since love is blind, we often keep one—or both—eyes shut during court-ship. We want to see the future as being full of possibilities and, therefore, tend to skip over the realities. Consider the man quoted at the beginning of the chapter who was dating a woman with six children (all teenagers!) while he himself had four children (mostly teenagers). They had been divorced and widowed respectively for less than two years and were dating long-distance (which would mean a significant physical move for one set of children should the couple decide to marry). Blinded by warm feelings of romance and the results from an online compatibility test (which didn't take into consideration the dynamics of children, loss, or the transitions of blending two families), these two parents moved forward rapidly with their relationship despite the fact that everything about their circumstances shouted for them to use caution or perhaps even put the relationship on hold. The idealism of love, you see, can easily lead us to overlook the reality of our circumstances and focus on what we dream will be.

COMMON UNREALISTIC EXPECTATIONS

Unrealistic expectations resulted in significant stumbling blocks for the couples in our research. For example, couples have many unrealistic expectations regarding the complex adjustments they will experience as their stepfamily tries to form a family identity.[1] Only 35 percent of unhappy couples in our study felt adequately prepared for the realities of stepfamily living; many of them hadn't even discussed and agreed on the responsibilities of raising children and stepchildren (46 percent). Ignorance is not bliss when it comes to marriage. It may be a welcome buffer before the wedding—shielding the couple from the realistic challenges of stepfamily living—but there's a real difference between optimism and foolish certainty.

When unrealistic expectations meet reality, disappointment sets in and becomes a huge relational obstacle for many couples. Once disillusionment is felt, persons tend to blame the relationship itself or their spouse instead of their own unrealistic expectations. When this happens, partners posture themselves against each other, not beside each other.

Anticipating or identifying unrealistic expectations, then, helps the common disappointments of marriage to simply become part of the terrain and not the fault of any one individual. Our research highlighted a number of key unrealistic expectations for you to consider.

Getting remarried and creating a stepfamily might be stressful, but what's the problem? We wish we had a dollar for every person who said, "Dating was so comfortable for us. Why has this marriage been so stressful?" Answer: because dating isn't real life; marriage is. Dating is about impressing the other person and putting forth our best effort. For example, couples are less defensive with each other before the wedding; but people relax and stop trying to impress each other after the wedding. In addition, future stepparents typically avoid taking disciplinary authority with children while dating the child's parent. After the wedding, however, stepparents begin to assert authority with stepchildren, which forces both of them into unknown—and often unwanted— territory with each other.[2]

Creating a stepfamily is, in fact, stressful, and many of the stressors aren't evident until after the wedding, even if you're looking for them. A full 88 percent of all the couples creating stepfamilies in our study disagreed about how stressful stepfamily living would be, or both anticipated that the complexities of stepfamily living would be stressful and difficult to manage. And they were right in assuming so. One study found that during the first few years after marriage, couples in stepfamilies report twice the level of stress reported by couples in first marriages.[3] It just seems to come with the territory. Therefore, don't assume the presence of stress is an indication of a poor marriage. Unfortunately, it is to be expected. But it can be managed with determination. The chapters on communication and managing conflict will help.

Let us emphasize here, though, that you need to agree and anticipate together that stepfamily living will bring added stress. If one partner acknowledges that stress is normal, but the other partner unrealistically believes that the family's adjustment will be easy, the couple is set up for disillusionment.

We identified key stumbling blocks for couples creating stepfamilies (see chapter 2 for a list of the top twelve). Stumbling blocks are items that one or both partners perceive as a problem. Some of the most significant perceived stumbling blocks for couples in our study pertained to stepfamily adjustment issues, including the children putting additional strain on their marriage (86 percent), creating a stepfamily putting more stress on their marriage

(85 percent), and the difficulties of adjusting to a stepfamily (78 percent). Stepfamily adjustment is stressful and can add strain to your marriage. Again, that is normal. If you face that truth divided, you will find managing the additional strain even more difficult. If, however, you face that truth together—as a team—you will support each other through the stress and find solutions to dilemmas more easily.

If we love each other, the children will follow close behind. The reality is that while your relationship does set the tone for all the other relationships in your home, it doesn't order them. In other words, without a healthy marriage, the stepfamily has little chance of succeeding, but even with a healthy couple relationship, the stepfamily as a whole can struggle. The attitudes and adjustments of children can operate quite independently of the couple's relational success. Therefore, having realistic expectations regarding the children is very important.

Some children might naturally welcome the new family, others will gradually adapt to it, and still others might resist it. Strong stepcouples don't panic when resistance becomes apparent; neither do they attempt to fix their child's concerns with simple words like "I'm sure you'll learn to accept Toni soon; after all, she loves you very much." Instead, they accept where each child is at a given moment in time and continue to build relationships between stepparents and stepchildren over time. Expecting the family to take a great deal of time to bond is more realistic and allows couples to relax as the family unit finds its way.

If we are in love and our marriage is strong, children, outside forces, and ex-spouses will not divide us. Former spouses do interfere with stepcouples, as do extended family members and children from previous marriages. For example, when we compared high-quality (happy) stepcouple relationships to low-quality (unhappy) ones, we found that only 54 percent of unhappy partners felt secure in their marriage when their spouse spent time with his or her children. However, 82 percent of couples in high-quality relationships were unified in feeling secure even when their partner was with his or her children. It seems that the perception of children as a barrier to the marriage creates a barrier even if one wouldn't exist otherwise.

It is important to accept that, in addition to children, forces outside the family will influence family life. Stepparents, for example, should strive to accept that at times a mate's ex-spouse will have more influence over their family's daily schedule than they do. Biological parents usually strive to represent their new families when negotiating with ex-spouses, but at the same time they are sometimes accommodating to their exes in order to reduce conflict in front of the children. This may mean that they—and their new spouse—will have to make sacrifices on behalf of the children.

There is, of course, an important balance to be sought. Biological parents must intentionally seek to manage boundaries around their marriages so that external forces (e.g., ex-spouses) and commitments to children don't completely sabotage time given to the marriage. Each has its place.

Emotional resolution of previous losses and painful relationships means they won't affect us in the future. Many individuals who go through a divorce recovery program are often surprised to discover that a "dead and buried past" is easily resurrected. Fears and assumptions based on previous relationships can color how partners view new relationships; if left unchecked, this can easily destroy the new marriage (see the next section on relationship concerns). Moving on doesn't mean your—or your mate's—baggage is left behind. One woman discovered her husband's baggage through his comparisons. *"Before marriage he told me what was wrong with his first wife. After we married, he compared me to what she did right."* Fears and leftover baggage are significant stumbling blocks for couples. And they are very common. Nearly two-thirds (63 percent) of all couples in our study sometimes fear another relationship breakup, and 58 percent don't think both partners have worked through all the issues and hurts from past relationships.

===== **Relationship Concerns in** =====
Happy and Unhappy Stepcouple Marriages

1. Almost half of happy couples (45 percent) are no longer fearful of another relationship breakup, while 81 percent of unhappy couples are.

2. Only 18 percent of happy couples feel left out when their spouse spends time with their children. Nearly half of unhappy ones do (46 percent).

3. Only 10 percent of happy couples have concerns about differences in sexual desire and their partner's previous sexual experiences. Around 40 to 50 percent of unhappy couples share these concerns.

4. Fifty percent of unhappy couples believe their partner is too influenced by his or her family or previous partner. Only 10 percent of happy couples worry about this.

5. Jealousy is an issue for only 11 percent of happy couples, but it affects 56 percent of unhappy ones.

High-quality relationships, by contrast, are characterized by couples who manage their fears and emotional baggage from the past. Three times as many healthy couples (61 percent) agree that each partner has worked through the issues and hurts related to their past compared to unhappy couples (only 21 percent). Furthermore, in a healthy couple, partners aren't overly bothered when their mate talks about a previous relationship. A significant 79 percent of healthy couples accept their mate's previous relationship history while just 44 percent of unhealthy couples do. This, combined with a fear of another relationship breakup (held by 81 percent of unhealthy couples), creates high relationship concerns and a low confidence in the future marriage.

RELATIONSHIP CONCERNS

Confidence in marriage is important. It nurtures a positive attitude toward your spouse and a high motivation to find positive ways of relating. Fear and concern, however, erode how we receive our mate's words and actions, and it increases the likelihood that spouses will seek out evidence to support their suspicions. In Ron's book *The Smart Stepfamily: Seven Steps to a Healthy Family*, he refers to these as ghosts. The ghost of marriage past, if you will, can lead one partner to live as if negative things are happening when they're not, and he or she will interpret behaviors, attitudes, or words with meaning that was only justifiably attributable to the previous relationship.

Our research revealed that feelings of jealousy (e.g., the fear of being replaced), suspicion (e.g., having trouble believing your partner), worry (e.g., how your mate's previous sexual experiences compare to yours), and fear (e.g., afraid of another relationship breakup) predict with nearly 93 percent accuracy couples with high- versus low-quality relationships. Fears erode confidence and set the couple up to interpret benign behaviors in cancerous ways.

Couples who are intent on developing a long-lasting relationship should strive to manage their inner concerns and fears. Gary's wife, Shirley, complained that he wouldn't let her take any parental initiative with his children. Upon first reflection, Gary was aware that he struggled to release control of his kids, but he didn't know why. After exploring some of the couple's relational history, Gary's therapist uncovered that the pain of Gary's last wife's abandonment impacted his current marital concerns. The answer—and Gary's ghost—hit him right between the eyes.

He knew he had been holding on to his children in order to protect them from further pain, but what he didn't realize was that he was also protecting himself. Holding on to them meant he didn't have to give as much of himself to Shirley. He feared making himself vulnerable to hurt, and he worried that she might not be fully committed to the marriage. He discovered that he had been intentionally making his wife jealous of his children so he could be assured of her desire for him; the irony was that over time this inadvertently built resentment in Shirley's heart toward both him and his children. Instantly Gary realized that he had to wrestle with his own fears—he had to become a ghost buster!—instead of luring his wife into temporarily alleviating them with her jealous desire. When he faced his fears and learned to manage them, both he and his wife grew more confidence in their marriage.

FEAR AND COHABITATION

With fears of getting hurt and the desire to seek convenient ways of coupling, a majority of couples in America today are choosing to cohabit before remarriage.[4] The belief is that a "trial marriage" will help them make a final decision about marriage or protect them from harm. They are mistaken. Cohabitation before marriage actually increases the likelihood of relationship breakup even if the couple goes on to marry.

One young woman shared how her parents' two divorces and her first failed marriage led her to be extra cautious about dating. When her long-term boyfriend asked her to marry him, she suggested they just live together for a while to see how it goes. "I wasn't going to walk into another painful breakup," she said. "I'd rather be safe than sorry." And she isn't alone.

A study by Dr. Larry Bumpass[5] revealed that the current cohabitation rate in the U.S. before marriage is 70 percent. In other words, the first couple experience for 70 percent of people is cohabitation, not marriage.[6] And this trend shows no signs of slowing down. In 2000, a study found that 66 percent of high school senior boys and 61 percent of girls "agreed" or "mostly agreed" with the idea that living together before marriage is usually a good idea to find out whether the couple could really get along.[7] In addition, we believe we will see the post-divorce cohabitation rate continue to climb as people seek to protect themselves from emotional pain.

Why do people cohabit? Smoking cigarettes is very bad for your health, but people still do it. The same is true for cohabitation. Here is a list of reported reasons why couples cohabit.[8]

- Economic advantages: *"We can save money by sharing living expenses."*
- Increase intimacy: *"We have more opportunities to share sexual and emotional intimacy without getting married."*
- Testing compatibility: *"Living together enables us to better learn about each other's habits and character and see how we operate together day-to-day."*
- Trial marriage: *"We are planning to marry soon."*
- Less complicated dissolution: *"If the relationship doesn't work out, there is no messy divorce."*

It is this fear of divorce that is driving couples to a halfway-house approach. Conceivably, cohabitation allows couples to protect themselves from emotional pain while obtaining the economic and sexual benefits that normally are reserved for marriage. The fear of hurt is particularly high in pre-stepfamily couples who have themselves already felt the pain of an ended relationship (even if by death, but particularly if by divorce) and don't want to expose their children to more potential hurt should another marriage dissolve. The irony, however, is that cohabiting relationships experience the very thing they hope to guard against. The research is clear:[9]

- Cohabiting couples have lower levels of personal happiness and higher rates of depression than married couples.[10]
- Cohabiters value independence more than married partners and have more individual freedom.[11]
- Cohabiters are less likely to be supportive financially of each other than are married partners.[12]

- Cohabiting couples are less sexually committed or trustworthy.[13]
- Cohabiters have more negative attitudes about marriage than non-cohabiters.[14]
- Couples living together have the lowest level of premarital satisfaction when compared to other living arrangements.[15]
- Marriages preceded by cohabitation are more likely to end in divorce.[16]
- Cohabiters have lower scores than non-cohabiters on religious behaviors, personal faith, church attendance, and joint religious activities.
- Cohabiting increases the risk of couple abuse and, if there are children, child abuse.

Essentially, cohabitation is living with second best and then wondering why it didn't work out for the best. Is cohabitation a true test of a couple's potential marriage quality (i.e., trial marriage)? Does it help couples avoid a breakup before marriage or divorce after the wedding? Absolutely not. Yet couples still do it, even to the detriment of their relationship.

AN HONEST LOOK IN THE MIRROR

Unrealistic expectations and unnecessary fears are not easy to spot. Often they only become apparent when they give birth to behavioral patterns that create difficulties in the relationship. Once identified, it is crucial that you honestly examine how your expectations and fears are impacting your attitudes and behavior. To ignore them is to invite further erosion of the relationship.

COUPLE POSITIONING SYSTEM (CPS)

Where are you NOW? (Identify and Discuss Your Results)

a. Think again about your overall Checkup results.

- What does this tell you about the condition of your relationship now? Do you need to focus your efforts to improve it?

b. Consider each statement below and share how each expectation has affected your relationship.

- Getting remarried and creating a stepfamily might be stressful, but what's the problem?
- If we love each other, the children will follow close behind.
- If we are in love and our marriage is strong, children, outside forces, and ex-spouses will not divide us.
- Emotional resolution of previous losses and painful relationships means they won't affect us in the future.

Where would you like to be? (Discuss Issues)

a. Choose one unrealistic expectation that you believe needs to change.

b. Share how you each feel about this matter.

c. How might things be different when you no longer live with this unrealistic expectation?

How do you get there? (Develop Your Action Plan)

a. Brainstorm a list of ways to handle this issue.

b. Agree on one solution you will try.

c. Decide what you will each do to make the plan work.

d. Review the progress in one week.

Bonus: Take a few minutes to work through the Ghost Busting exercise on the following pages.

BONUS COUPLE EXERCISE
A CASE STUDY IN GHOST BUSTING

Once you realize that the pain of the past is leading you to have fears of the future, how do you deal with them? Sandra had no idea how powerful her concerns would be until she got remarried. Only then did her fears come to the surface. She was determined to take control of them and set them aside so they wouldn't limit her ability to give and receive in her marriage. She took our advice and created a chart comparing what her current fears led her to feel and how she would react when the fears were set aside. It looked like this:

The Fear Ghost: Current Fears and Reactions	New and Improved: Loving Without Limits
Triggers: • An angry scowl from her husband • Money missing from the bank account • Husband's lack of interest in her children • Conflict over insignificant things	*Triggers* (these won't change): • An angry scowl from her husband • Money missing from the bank account • Husband's lack of interest in her children • Conflict over insignificant things
Thoughts: • This is what preceded my last husband divorcing me; get prepared for the worst • Guard your heart; assume the worst • Protect the kids from his anger	*Thoughts:* • I don't know what his scowl means; I need to ask and listen • Give the benefit of the doubt; ask with an open mind • Wonder how we can work through this together
Feelings: • Insecure; fearful; cautious • Hurt; defensive; protective	*Feelings:* • Curious about his reactions; open to knowing and understanding more • Secure in his commitment even when temporarily angry

Actions:	Actions:
• Get quiet and don't share thoughts	• Talk; be available; listen to his complaints; share my frustrations
• Avoid discussing sensitive matters	• Be affectionate
• Jump between kids and husband	• Be assertive with concerns and working through conflicts
• Withhold affection	• Allow him room to build relationship with my children
	• Open to his parenting thoughts; we negotiate behavioral management of children together

Make a similar chart of your current fears, thoughts, and feelings; what you will think and feel; and how you will act when your fears are managed more effectively. Then share your chart with your spouse and ask him or her to help you move in the right direction. A spouse who is working with you will not use your fears against you, but will be compassionate about your desire to change. Read the New and Improved list many times each day to remind yourself of how you want to react. Celebrate the times that you notice a trigger and are able to act more appropriately to the situation instead of letting your fears take control. Change will not likely happen quickly or easily. However, a persistent effort on your part and an environment of love and support from your spouse can help to cast out the fear in your heart.

For more information on typical ghosts following the death of a spouse or a divorce, go to *www.SuccessfulStepfamilies.com/view/406*. If your mate has a ghost and you want to know how to help, this information will also be helpful.

Chapter 7

Children and Parenting:
When Kids Are Part of the Package

Hector and I are perfectly happy and our marriage is wonderful—when his girls are not around.

—Stepmother
Married three years

You may be wondering, *Why a chapter about children and parenting in a book about marriage?* Answer: Because when it comes to stepcoupling, children are a critical part of the marital package. Nothing impacts a stepcouple's relationship more than the presence of their children. In all marriages (first or subsequent), the couple's relationship sets the tone for parenting. But in a remarriage, what is equally true is that parenting sets the tone for couple happiness. For both men and women, there exists a strong correlation between couple happiness and stepfamily dynamics. In fact, the relationship is so strong that stepfamily issues account for 41 percent of what contributes to a husband's satisfaction level in the couple relationship and close to half (46 percent) of a wife's satisfaction level. Also, you may recall from chapter 2 that the top five specific concerns for remarrying couples are related to stepfamily adjustment and parenting issues.

But that is just part of the picture. We also found that stepfamily issues—most of which revolve around parenting matters—become more impacting on the couple relationship over time. Before the wedding, couple satisfaction is based more on the couple's interactions than the stepfamily "package." But after the wedding, parenting and stepfamily dynamics become even more salient to couple satisfaction and happiness. Even before the wedding, 86 percent of all couples in our study believed that children would put an additional strain on their marriage. They are right.

Julie wrote and asked a common question. "Why is it that Hector and I can't get along when his girls are here? When it's just the two of us, we enjoy each other. Hector and I are perfectly happy and our marriage is wonderful—when his girls are not around. But when they are here, we argue about parenting, discipline, and fairness. In the end, I end up feeling left out and sabotaged by him as a parent."

Previously we stated that the divorce rate for remarried couples (whether they have children from previous relationships or not) is at least 60 percent (73 percent for third marriages).[1] We also noted that stepcouples in particular (those who bring children into the marriage) have a 50 percent higher chance of divorce than remarriages that don't bring children to the marriage. What's the difference? Why is marriage in a stepfamily more difficult? We believe a significant part of it stems from the varying relational attachments between parents, stepparents, and children and the complications of forming relationships after loss and combining different family histories, parenting styles, and expectations for the children's behavior. That's why Hector and Julie find it more difficult to be a family than to just be a couple.

COMMITTED LOVE

You may be in love with your spouse, but is it *committed love*? One woman commented, "I just can't stand having my children feel left out. They are my kids and I'm not going to let some man get in the way of our relationship." In other words, she was saying that she is in love with her husband, but not fully committed to him. In fact, it sounds like she is more committed to her children than to him. Barring a miracle, this marriage is headed for distress, at best, and possibly divorce unless she has a change of heart.

Marriage is too important to go at it halfheartedly. Individuals who choose to cherish their children over their marriage are asking for a host of problems. Kids in this situation instinctively know they have more power in the home than the stepparent; all they have to do is whine and their parent comes to their defense. This breeds resentment, jealousy, hurt, anger, and competition throughout the stepfamily.

Making the marriage the priority relationship, then, paradoxically invites children to gain respect for the stepparent, and it empowers the stepparent to actually care for the children in loving and sacrificial ways because they aren't in competition with them. Yet making the marriage a priority may feel to the biological parent like having an appendectomy without anesthesia. It can hurt the children's feelings, and if children express anger over feeling displaced or insecure with the transition, that can increase the biological parent's guilt and anxiety about the children's well-being.

Now, before you fear that we're asking biological parents to abandon their children for the sake of the marriage, let us be perfectly clear: Making the marriage a significant priority does not mean you neglect your children, nor that your spouse gets to be the total focus of your attention. Loving your spouse should never come at the expense of the children. In general it means that you seek a balance between the love and energy you give your children with what's necessary to sustain and build your marriage. More specifically it means that if push comes to shove, you make it clear to your children that your marriage will last above all else.

In healthy first marriages, this notion typically goes without saying, since the marriage preceded the children. The couple and children inherently know that "Mom and Dad started this thing together, and they're going to finish it together." Plus—and this is what really separates stepcouple marriages from first marriages—children in biological families don't feel threatened when their parents' marriage is strengthened. In fact, they rejoice in it. As of the writing of this chapter, my (Ron's) parents have been married for fifty-two years. As a child I may have squirmed a little when they hugged in the kitchen after dinner, but I wasn't offended or threatened by it. If anything, I felt a security in my life because of it. But in stepfamilies, children often feel a great sense of loss when their parent's new marriage is strengthened. It threatens their sense of family and the often-held fantasy of a parental reconciliation. Children typically don't rejoice when stepcouples fall in love (especially during the first few years), and when they do feel positively about the marriage, it still causes them confusion. In addition, your courtship and decision to marry creates another emotional transition (remember, even before the wedding children have already experienced a number of painful transitions), which requires mental, spiritual, and emotional resolution.

Even with the awareness that your marriage transition generates insecurity and anxiety in children, couples must openly declare and demonstrate their commitment to the marriage in order to establish themselves as the foundation to the home. It is the first step toward marital intimacy, stepfamily harmony, and effective parenting.

Children who witness their parent's obvious dedication to their new spouse understand that respecting their parent includes respecting their choice of mate. Without a strong commitment from the biological parent, most children are not motivated to accept the stepparent's presence, let alone authority.

Paula and her husband have been remarried for fifteen years. "We absolutely love our family now, but I must tell you it wasn't always much fun," she commented. When asked to reflect back and think about when their family turned the corner toward peace and harmony, she said, "It was when all five of our children came to believe and accept that our marriage wasn't going away. It took each child a different amount of time—the oldest two had the most trouble with this—but once they finally accepted it, things got much better."

Marital commitment is a significant first step toward providing a foundation for growth in the stepfamily home, including managing the children. Yet even then, parenting in stepfamilies comes with complications and stumbling blocks.

PARENTING IN STEPFAMILIES: STUMBLING BLOCKS AND STRENGTHS

For most of us, our parenting style is heavily influenced by the family we grew up in. The more similar the parenting styles of both your parents, the more likely it is that you will see eye to eye on discipline strategies, the amount and type of rules to set, and the level of emotional involvement you want to have in your children's lives.

Parenting Strengths of Happy vs. Unhappy Couples		
	Percent of Happy Couples	Percent of Unhappy Couples
Have concerns about the kind of parent or stepparent my spouse will be.	6%	40%
Have discussed the responsibilities of raising children and stepchildren.	84%	54%
My partner's family raised children in a similar manner to mine.	69%	6%
We have agreed on how to discipline our children/stepchildren.	68%	36%
We agree on the type of religious education for our children/stepchildren.	74%	44%

Eighty-two percent of all couples acknowledge that they were parented differently as a child than their spouse was. This can become a significant stumbling block for stepcouples unless they negotiate toward a unified posture in parenting. In addition, becoming a unified team in parenting is complicated by the fact that children are often invested in their parent's parenting style as well. That is, they too are used to a system of parenting and expectations, and may feel resentful if the presence of a stepparent brings changes. Furthermore, parents who during the single-parent years grew used to managing their children without help from others may find it very difficult to release control to the stepparent (even though they want them included). This is why it is critical that couples discuss and agree to a system of behavioral management for the children.

One of the strengths of very happy couples in our study was their ability to come together around matters of child-rearing. Happy couples (84 percent) had discussed their responsibilities, and 68 percent had agreed on how to discipline the children; much fewer unhappy or dissatisfied couples had (54 percent and 36 percent respectively). And, for example, 74 percent of strong stepcouples came to an agreement on the type of religious education they wanted their children and stepchildren to receive. Couples who find consensus regarding behavioral discipline and expectations grow closer together and are much better equipped to manage the various emotions demonstrated by the children.

THREE KEYS TO PARENTING IN STEPFAMILIES

Key 1: Biological Parents Must Pass Authority to Stepparents

Rules without relationship brings rebellion.[2] The main challenge to stepparenting is earning or building a relationship with a stepchild that affords the stepparent the needed authority to make rules and impose consequences for disobedience.[3] Until such a relationship is built and trust between stepparent and stepchild established, how is a stepparent supposed to gain authority? As John and Emily Visher so wisely pointed out many years ago, they must live on borrowed power from the biological parent.[4]

Parents pass authority to the stepparent when they make it clear to their children that the stepparent is an extension of their authority. Saying something like, "I know Bob is not your dad, but when I am not here, he will be enforcing the household rules we have agreed on. I expect you to be courteous and respect him as you would any authority figure," communicates your expectations clearly. Be sure then to back up the stepparent just like you would a baby-sitter or your child's teacher at school. We'll say more about relationship and authority in a moment.

Key 2: Biological Parents Should Build Trust in Stepparents

One of the greatest barriers to entrusting your children to your spouse is a fundamental lack of trust in the stepparent's intentions. In a two-parent biological home, couples don't seem to question the motives of their spouse. They may not agree with the specific parenting decisions of their spouse, but they don't question their spouse's love or commitment to the child. Parents generally assume the best about the other biological parent's motives. Stepparents are not always granted that same benefit of the doubt.

Roger loved Cheryle very much, but he just wasn't sure why she was critical of his two daughters. Cheryle complained that Roger was too easy on them and she feared they would grow up to be "spoiled, boy-chasing girls." Roger believed that Cheryle's real problem was jealousy; he interpreted her criticism of the girls as her attempt to step between Roger and his daughters. Therefore he ignored her input and discounted her efforts at discipline.

In order to give your spouse the benefit of the doubt, you must force yourself to trust her motives. Sometimes stepparents *are* jealous, but that doesn't mean they are mean-spirited toward your children. If you don't strive for trust, you'll continually defend your children, even when ill-advised. Your children will learn that obeying the stepparent is optional (since you'll stick up for them), and your spouse will truly grow to resent your children. Open yourself to the stepparent's input and trust their heart. Talk, listen, and negotiate.

Key 3: Stepparents Should Move Into Relationship and Discipline Gradually

Since authority is based on relationship and trust with the child, stepparents should move gradually into relationship first, then discipline. Researcher James Bray says one of the most important step-parenting skills after remarriage is *monitoring the children's activities*.[5] The focus of monitoring is strengthening relationship with the child. It involves knowing their daily routines, where they are, who they are with, and what extracurricular activities they are involved in, but does not necessarily include being involved in the child's emotional life. It is parenting that is sensitive to the pace of the child—not pushing too hard for closeness, but continually being an active presence in the child's life in order to allow for relationship to grow. Monitoring step-parents check homework and daily chores and befriend stepchildren, yet refrain from emotional closeness that is unwelcome to the child. Bottom line: Good stepparents listen to the child's level of openness, and they keep trying to nurture a relationship with their stepchildren, even if they are rejected again and again. They are persistent and gracious. And in the end, much of the time, a connection is created that is beneficial to the child, the stepparent, and the marriage.

Once a stronger bond is built between stepparent and stepchild, a natural authority to teach, train, and discipline begins to grow.

There are two kinds of authority: positional authority and relational authority. Positional authority is what your boss at work has over you, and it's what a teacher has in the classroom. Their position in that context gives them authority. Relational authority is much more influential—and difficult to obtain—because it is afforded someone who has the trust of another. Caring about your boss's evaluation because you're hoping for a raise is one thing; caring about his opinion because as friends you have come to care about each other is another.

Stepparents come into the stepfamily with positional authority. That is, because they are an adult, they are afforded some authority as is any adult, teacher, or neighbor. When children come to care about the stepparent as a person and value their relationship, then a stepparent has gained relational authority. Positional authority is dependent upon the biological parent's backing; relational authority stands on its own. Obviously, relational authority is an attractive goal for stepparents, but it must be earned the old-fashioned way—by nurturing a relationship with the child. A stepparent who walks into a family claiming the rights of relational authority without having earned them frequently finds hostility from the children (or at least one child) and resentment from their spouse for being heavy-handed.

A child's trust, respect, and honor grow out of a relational history with a stepparent that comes with time and positive experiences. Successful stepparents are dedicated to relationship building over the long haul and don't try to force their way into the child's heart. They also understand the limitations of positional authority in the first few years of the stepfamily and rely heavily on the biological parent to manage the children until their own relational influence grows.[6]

Helen called to complain about her husband's parenting of her son. "Larry's not abusive, but he will always say no to whatever Brandon asks. When Larry walks into the room, he always tells Brandon to do chores or some task. Larry just won't open himself up to Brandon. I feel like I am always running defense for my son, and it is the biggest cause of fights in my marriage." Larry was critical and non-accepting of his stepson, and it was pushing both his stepson and his wife away. Larry needed to learn ways of connecting with his stepson. Taking a humble attitude and being willing to engage Brandon in his interests, sharing talents and skills with Brandon that they might have in common, complimenting Brandon, and showing appreciation for how he contributes to the home are just a few ideas he could implement.

Second chances. When mistakes have been made, stepparents need to find the courage to back off and try a different approach. One mom's fiancé, a retired Marine, called her before their wedding and made an announcement. "You tell your kids that once we get married, the Marines have landed!" He was declaring that her children better be prepared for his rules and discipline once he married their mother. Was that well received? Hardly. I (Ron) caught up with the mother a few years later and asked what the outcome had been. Their household had been filled with hurt, anger, and disillusionment for the first couple years, but to her husband's credit, he realized how misguided he had been and backed off. He apologized for demanding love and authority he hadn't earned, and let his wife take over the role of primary parent. His apology gave the family a chance to heal and to start over. Sometimes you just need a second chance.

BE THE BEST PARENT YOU CAN BE

So far we've established that in order to protect your marriage, the parenting unit comprised of a biological parent and stepparent needs to be unified in mutual support for each other. This empowers you to lead your family from a position of unity and, in cooperation with an effective parenting style, will add considerable harmony to the marriage and family.

Styles of Parenting

Differing ideas about how best to parent is an issue for 64 percent of unhappy stepcouples. Surprisingly it's also an issue for about one-third of happily married couples. Let's review the different styles of parenting and which one works best.[7]

PARENTING STYLES and Family Map

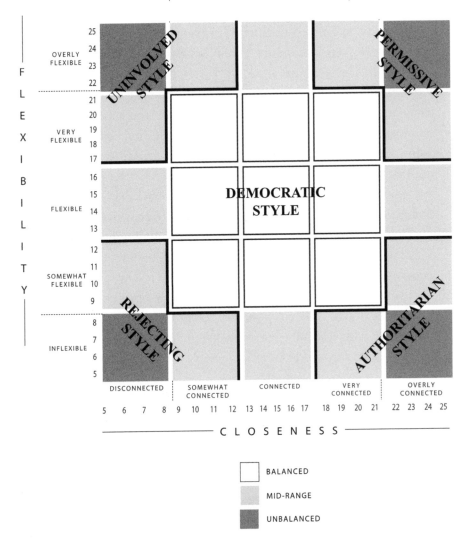

Democratic parenting. Sometimes referred to as authoritative, these parents establish clear rules and expectations and discuss them with the child. Although they acknowledge the child's perspective, they use both reason and power to enforce their standards. On the Parenting Styles and Family Map, democratic parenting represents a balance of closeness and flexibility. Connected parents have solid, loving relationships with their children. This provides the child a safe environment with unconditional support, encouragement, and affection. The balanced flexibility of the home also provides structure, clear expectations, and limits. When behavioral lines are crossed, children are firmly admonished, but love remains.

Considerable research on parenting has demonstrated that more democratic parents have children who are more emotionally healthy and happy, are more successful in school and life, and have a greater value-based outlook on life. They are cheerful, are self-reliant, cope with stress well, and are achievement oriented.[8]

Authoritarian parenting. These parents have more rigid rules and expectations and strictly enforce them. They expect and demand obedience from their children. The authoritarian style is located in the lower right quadrant of the Family Map and is characterized by very structured to rigid parenting while closeness and loyalty to the family are highly demanded. The more extreme this type of parenting is, the more difficulty for children, especially adolescents, who tend to rebel against it. Children of authoritarian parents are often conflicted, irritable in behavior, moody and unhappy, vulnerable to stress, and unfriendly.

Parenting Styles and Children's Behavior

Parenting Style	Typical Child Behavior
Democratic	Energetic and friendly Self-reliant and cheerful Achievement oriented
Authoritarian	Unfriendly Conflicted and irritable Unhappy and unstable
Permissive	Impulsive and rebellious Low achieving
Rejecting	Immature Psychologically troubled
Uninvolved	Lonely and withdrawn Low achieving

Permissive parenting. These parents let the child's preferences take priority over the parents' ideals, and they rarely force the child to confirm to reasonable behavioral standards. Expectations and rules are chaotic at times and are easily manipulated because these parents prefer to keep the peace with their children. A warm, affectionate friendship with the child is the parent's most important priority even though it results in impulsive-aggressive children who are often rebellious, domineering, and low achievers.

Rejecting parenting. These parents do not pay much attention to their child's needs but have high expectations regarding how the child should behave. These families have little emotional connection; children are not sure they are loved due to the parents' disengaged style. An environment with high expectations and little emotional support creates children who feel they aren't good enough; failure comes with great insecurity and shows itself in low self-esteem, immaturity, and a variety of psychological problems.

Uninvolved parenting. Also called neglectful parenting, these parents often ignore the child, letting the child's preferences prevail as long as they do not interfere with the parents' activities. Like the rejecting parent, uninvolved parents are emotionally disengaged, but they don't have rigid rules or expectations. Rather, they are overly flexible in their structure, leaving the child alone without consistent boundaries. Children of uninvolved parents are often withdrawn loners and low achievers.

WORKING TOGETHER

Obviously, the most optimal parenting style is the democratic or authoritative (not to be confused with authoritarian) style. However, for stepparents, choosing this style is a matter of timing. In her stepfamily curriculum *Smart Steps,* Dr. Francesca Adler-Baeder points out that because stepparents enter the family without a relationship upon which to base authority or discipline, they should choose first to operate from a "supportive" parenting role. She suggests that stepparents initially focus on two behavioral goals: (1) supporting the biological parent as *primary* authority to the children; and (2) building a trust-bond relationship with their stepchildren. Since the stepparent is intentionally not moving into a disciplinary role, this may sound like a recipe for disaster. But remember that the stepparent is prescribed this role only in the early months or years of the marriage. When the biological parent leads from a position of strength as a democratic parent, the stepparent can afford to focus less on discipline and more on relationship building. The advantage of the supportive role for the stepparent is the ability to softly enter the child's life, first as a friend, then mentor, then parent. Over time, as a relationship bond builds, stepparents will gradually shift into a democratic style of parenting with some stepchildren. This may never happen with older or part-time stepchildren who have less time in the home, but it can be optimal with younger children. Again, it's a matter of timing.

A true disaster for everyone in the home is when the biological parent historically has parented with any style other than democratic and continues to do so after the wedding. This sets the stepparent up for failure because the lack of structure or love in the home leads the stepparent to act in ways that may not be well received. Biological parents must honestly examine their parenting history and current approach to parenting. If it is anything less than democratic, we strongly encourage you to "fill the gaps" in your home by adopting a more democratic parenting style. Doing so will help the stepparent establish themselves in the home and eventually bless children with a more effective child-rearing environment.

GUARD YOUR MARRIAGE

On the stepfamily map, at the intersection of Parenting Street and Marriage Avenue, is a Caution sign that reads, "Guard Your Marriage." Parenting dilemmas in stepfamilies have the potential to undermine and sabotage the health of your marriage. Carefully protect your marriage by working together as a team to lead the children in your care. Work hard to lead from a position of unity, support each other in front of the children, and parent effectively with the biological parent using a democratic style and the stepparent adapting their style from "permissive" toward democratic over time. Couples who miss the Caution sign can easily find themselves in a head-on collision, calling 9-1-1. Don't be a casualty. Buckle up and proactively guard your marriage.

COUPLE POSITIONING SYSTEM (CPS)

Where are you NOW? (Identify and Discuss Your Results)

a. Review the Couple Checkup Individual Results.

- How satisfied were each of you in this area?

b. Review the Couple Checkup Couple Results.

- Was it a Strength or Growth Area?

c. Discuss your Agreement items—these are your strengths.

d. Share your perspectives on the following items. Consider each privately to yourself. Then listen to your spouse's perspective, being sure you fully understand before offering your own.

- If someone were to ask your children whether they believed your marriage would last a lifetime, what would they say?

- What evidence would they use to support their answer?

- What complications does your marriage experience related to children and parenting?

- In what ways does making your marriage a priority cause you to feel guilty regarding your children?

- What might balancing time and energy between nurturing your marriage and loving/training your children look like?

- When it comes to the behavioral discipline of your children, do you share a common expectation and discipline strategy?

- If issues related to making your marriage a priority have arisen, set aside some time to discuss how you can begin elevating each other's status in front of the children.

Where would you like to be? (Discuss Issues)

a. Review the Discussion Items in your Couple Checkup Report.

b. Choose one issue that you both want to resolve.

c. Share how you each feel about the issue.

d. Look again at the list of parenting matters on which you don't agree. Decide which topics are priority matters for you and plan a time to negotiate your position as a couple. Try to find a position you can both support. It's always helpful to read a good parenting book together, attend a local parent education program, or consult a family therapist if you cannot resolve your differences.

How do you get there? (Develop Your Action Plan)

a. Brainstorm a list of ways to handle this issue.

b. Agree on one solution you will try.

c. Decide what you will each do to make the plan work.

d. Review the progress in one week.

e. Continue to build on your couple strengths. Remember, it's easier to build on strengths than to change frail aspects of your relationship.

- What positive things do you need to continue?

Chapter 8

SCOPE Out Your Personalities
With Peter J. Larson, PhD

*I love you not because of who you are, but because of who I am when
I am with you.*

—Roy Croft
Twentieth-century poet

Personality differences can be a challenge for many couples. We often
feel that our own style and approach to life is best. But differences
in personality can be a strength in your relationship; it just takes
awareness and effort.

We have created the SCOPE personality scale, which explores
five core personality characteristics. Your personality profile is summarized in your Couple Report, as is how you and your partner's
personalities interact. SCOPE is an acrostic: S stands for how social
you are, C stands for how you handle change, O measures how
organized you are, P is for how pleasing you are, and E looks at your
emotional stability.

PERSONALITY HAS MANY DEFINITIONS

There are many ways to describe personality, and the academic definition differs greatly from what is usually thought of when we say a person has "personality." Actually, personality is much broader and encompasses the entirety of an individual's feelings, behaviors, and preferences. It is helpful to think of personality as the characteristics of a person that lead to consistent patterns of feeling, thinking, and behaving.[1] This definition, while simple, generally provides a good framework from which to understand personality.

Personality characteristics are rather stable over time in most people. A common misperception is that you can change personality traits if you don't like them. While we might achieve slight adjustments in personality over time, our personality is pretty much set by adolescence. For example, a goal-oriented person with high organizational abilities will exhibit these traits in many settings over a lifetime. They may never feel comfortable just letting things slide or doing something in a sloppy or careless way. No one should expect their partner to change their personality traits. Skills can be learned and improved. An individual can learn to communicate or manage finances more effectively. But an introvert should not be expected to become an extrovert. An emotional person will likely always feel things more intensely than his less emotional partner. Couples who set out to change each other's personality will embark on a journey of frustration.

Harry and Joan had been married for several years. Harry loved to come home and have some downtime. He often felt the need to "zone out" for a while, with limited conversation and activity. Watching a movie or reading a book was a natural way for him to relax and recharge; it was just what his introverted personality craved. Harry's wife, Joan, had recently transitioned from her professional career to staying home with the baby. By the time the weekend arrived, she often felt isolated and longed for adult conversation and contact. For her, recharging involved social interaction and visiting with friends and family. She often invited others over for dinner or arranged an outing for she and Harry to meet with friends. For Joan, talking and laughing with lots of friends around was what her extroverted personality longed for.

While dating, this difference in personality had been something that originally attracted them to each other. Harry appreciated Joan's energy and ability to talk to anybody. She had many friends and got him out of the house. Joan was impressed with how thoughtful and deep Harry was. He seemed very mature and down to earth. But as is often the case, personality differences that initially attract eventually attack. As Harry and Joan's marriage progressed, these personality differences often led to conflict, misunderstandings, and hurt feelings. Joan would make plans with friends, only to have Harry push back, refusing "another outing." Joan couldn't figure out why he was always saying no to her fun plans. Harry didn't understand why Joan couldn't appreciate a quiet afternoon just relaxing with a book. More and more, they started to drift apart as Joan would go out with her friends in the evenings and weekends, leaving Harry home alone with the baby.

APPRECIATING PERSONALITY DIFFERENCES

If we can't change each other's personality, what do we do with our differences? Before Harry and Joan took their online Couple Checkup, they did not really understand and appreciate their personality differences. Their tendency was that of most individuals: trying to make the other person think, feel, and behave the right way—more like them. It is very easy to slip into a critical mode when your partner displays very different lifestyle preferences and behavior.

- *Why does she get so upset about little things?*
- *Why is he always losing things?*
- *Why does she always want to do things with others?*
- *How can a person get so excited about every new idea that comes along?*
- *Why does he want to change things all the time?*

We can learn a lot about the value of different skills by looking at a team. A good team is made up of individuals with strengths and abilities that are different from one another's. A good baseball team not only needs a pitcher who throws well, but also players who can hit and catch the ball. Great football teams not only have a solid quarterback leading the offense but also those who can run, catch, block, and tackle. Marriage represents another type of team that requires a range of skills and responsibilities to be successful. Rather than focusing on the ways we wish we were more alike or the things we'd like to change in each other, couples can learn to understand, appreciate, and work with their personality differences. Let the more organized person tackle the task of balancing the checkbook. Allow the more assertive person to negotiate a major purchase. While the person who loves change and new ideas will keep you up-to-date, the more conventional person can help your team stay grounded and make balanced decisions.

There is no right or wrong combination of personality traits to form a successful relationship. While some couples may have an easier time blending their styles and preferences, in the end, how you communicate, respect, and work with each other's differences will determine your relationship compatibility. Remember, your personality differences can be advantageous as you each bring unique abilities and perspectives to the relationship. Don't fall into the trap of criticizing each other's personality traits or trying to change someone to be something they are not. Instead, identify and discuss your similarities and differences and create solutions that allow you to work *with* each other rather than *against* each other.

Rather than just tolerate your personality differences, celebrate them. In his book *Sustaining Love,* David Augsburger points out that on the way to mature love, most couples go through four stages. First, during courtship, couples *accommodate* or tolerate each other's differences to avoid conflict and keep alive their dream relationship. After the wedding, when the reality of a spouse's personality sets in, partners try to *eliminate* the objectionable differences by criticizing or demanding change. However, when couples reach the third stage, they begin to *appreciate* the differences in personality as creative, necessary parts of the person they love *and* of the marriage itself. This paves the way for mature partners with a mature love to then *celebrate* and delight in their differences, recognizing that each is acceptable and beneficial to the health of the relationship.[2]

FINDING A BALANCE IN PERSONALITY

We've all seen people with extreme or out-of-balance personality styles: the person who is so painfully shy she cannot make eye contact or hold a conversation; the guy who loves to party but can't seem to hold a job; the friend who is so obsessed with religious activity that he neglects those around him; the relative who descends into anxiety or depression when things get stressful; or the person who stays up all night engaged in philosophical discussions on the future of politics—only to forget that important meeting or appointment the next morning. We should not use the fact that personality is made up of relatively stable traits as an excuse for extreme or disruptive behavior in our lives.

The concept of *balance* applies not only to the flexibility and closeness in relationships, but also to personality functioning. Once individuals understand their personality traits, they have the opportunity to begin making choices to ensure their behavior remains in balance. There is nothing wrong with being an introvert, but losing all contact with others or slipping into an aloof or alienated existence is out of balance. There is nothing wrong with being organized and goal-directed, but neglecting one's relationships with spouse or children so you can focus on nothing but work or school is out of balance. On a basic level, a personality trait is out of balance when it begins to interfere with work, school, or your personal life or relationships. Ask yourself, "Are there ways in which my personality is out of balance and interfering with other aspects of my life? What do I need to do to bring it back into balance?" You can even ask your partner what he or she thinks about the aspects of your personality that could be extreme. The Couple Checkup not only identifies your personality traits and styles, but helps to define what an unbalanced personality trait looks like.

Not everyone has areas of their personality that push over into the extremes. But if you have a personality area that needs to be brought back into balance, begin to strategize and make behavioral choices that will help you avoid extreme expressions of that trait. Set realistic goals that will lead to more balanced behavior. For the couple described earlier in this chapter, Harry and Joan's new understanding of their personalities led to productive compromise they could both feel good about. They decided that Joan could plan one social function for them to participate in as a couple each weekend. Joan agreed to make sure to leave one weekend day/night where Harry had plenty of downtime to recharge in the ways he preferred.

SCOPE IS BASED ON THE MOST VALID PERSONALITY APPROACH

SCOPE is based on what is often considered to be the most robust and highly researched model of personality in the world of psychology, the Five Factor Model.[3] Unlike other personality assessments, which are driven by a theoretical model of how personality is organized, the Five Factor Model began with no theory in mind. Instead, researchers conducted statistical analyses of every adjective in the English language to see what patterns or "factors" emerged. The resulting five factors have now been replicated in many other languages and cultures.

The SCOPE categories are designed to be positive and easy to understand. The following table provides an overview of what a high score means in each SCOPE category.

SCOPE Personality Profile Categories				
Social	Change	Organized	Pleasing	Emotion- ally Steady
Extro- verted vs. Introverted	Open to Change vs. Conven- tional	Consci- entious vs. Less Organized	Agreeable vs. Forceful	Calm vs. Reactive
• Skilled in handling social situations • The life of the party • Com- fortable around people • Makes friends easily • Often on the go • Loves large parties • Doesn't mind being center of attention	• Prefers variety to routine • Likes to begin new things • Enjoys vis- iting new places • Values flexibility • Enjoys thinking of new ways to do things • Comfort- able with change	• Always prepared • Makes plans and sticks with them • Carries out plans • Seldom wastes time • Gets chores and tasks done right away • Likes order • Tries to follow the rules	• Respects others • Doesn't like to be pushy • Believes in the good intentions of others • Accepts people as they are • Values coopera- tion over competition • Loves to help others • Has a good word for everyone	• Not easily bothered by things • Seldom gets mad • Rarely complains • Seldom feels blue • Comfort- able in unfamiliar situations • Feels com- fortable with self • Remains calm under pressure

SOCIAL

This trait considers one's behavior in regard to social situations.

High Social Scores: Those who score high on this scale are more extroverted. They enjoy being with people and are often full of energy. Such individuals tend to be enthusiastic and action-oriented. In groups, they like to talk, assert themselves, and may often be the center of attention. When out of balance, they can appear to be attention seeking or shallow. Others may even see high extroversion as an inability to take life seriously.

If you both score high on the Social scale, you are likely a very outgoing and energetic couple, poised for lots of fun. People are likely drawn to you because of your fun-loving mindset and ability to make friends easily. Potential drawbacks include becoming overly busy and too involved in outside activities. You may neglect placing enough priority on your couple relationship due to your busy social calendar. When out of balance, this leaves less time for your personal life and couple relationship. You may benefit from periodically scheduling time to reconnect alone with your partner.

Average Social Scores: Those who score in the average range may find social settings enjoyable but will value privacy as well. Their preference for being in groups or alone may change based on their mood or external circumstances. When both individuals in the couple score in this range, they generally enjoy having a balance between alone time and social activity.

Low Social Scores: Those who score low on the social scale tend to be reserved or introverted. Social introverts often lack the exuberance and activity levels of extroverts. They tend to be low-key, deliberate, and less connected socially. They often prefer to be alone or with just a few close friends. They will feel more energized after spending time alone or in small, intimate settings, as opposed to large groups or parties. When out of balance, they appear reclusive or cut off from others. Some people may even misinterpret the need for personal time as aloofness.

When both individuals of the couple score low on the social trait, they will be more reserved and private, enjoying quiet and relaxing time alone. Often, they do not enjoy going to large social gatherings. These events may cause more stress than enjoyment. A potential drawback is the possibility of becoming isolated and cut off from others. When out of balance, two social introverts can even feel isolated from each other. They will need to find ways of connecting with each other while still allowing the other the chance to recharge alone.

Handling Differences: When one partner is highly social and the other is not, the couple will need to communicate openly with each other about attending social events and getting together with others. One of them gets energy from socializing with others, while the other prefers more privacy and alone time. Unnecessary conflict can be avoided in these relationships by checking it out with the other partner before saying yes or no to participating in a social function.

CHANGE

This trait reflects your openness to change, flexibility, and interest in new experiences.

High Change Scores: Those who score in the high range will tend to be more flexible, unconventional, and very open to new experiences. They are open to change and often have a broad range of interests. Such individuals thrive on coming up with new and creative solutions to problems, even when a tried and true method might work just as well. When out of balance, they may appear to be overly interested in new ideas and adventures, forgetting more practical realities.

When both individuals of the couple score high on this dimension, they are likely to enjoy change in their lives. They sometimes need to be careful not to create too much change and unnecessary stress in their lives. Remember that the practical or conventional approach is sometimes the tried and true method, worthy of sticking with.

Average Change Scores: Those in the average range often strike a good balance between new, abstract, or creative ideas and more traditional or down-to-earth approaches to life. Based on the situations they encounter, they may fluctuate between being flexible or taking a "business as usual" approach. Couples who score in the average range are often practical but still open to considering new ideas when appropriate.

Low Change Scores: Individuals with low change scores are more down to earth, practical in nature, and less interested in new ideas and experiences. Change may be difficult for them and it may increase their stress level. They prefer the familiar and approaches they already understand and are accustomed to. Attitudes are likely to be more conventional or traditional. When out of balance, these individuals can appear rigid or closed off to new experiences.

When both individuals score low in change, they will present themselves as practical and more conventional in their attitudes. Neither person will rock the boat or create unnecessary stress by embracing a new approach to life. These couples may need to guard against letting their lives and relationship become too routine or boring.

Handling Differences: One partner scoring higher than the other in the change trait may represent a case of being attracted to one's opposite. The more practical person is often attracted to their partner's free thinking and open attitudes. Conversely, the more open partner may recognize the value of the other's steady approach to life. There will be times when each other's attitudes, preferences, or behavior will be challenging and lead to frustration. They will need to remember to work with their differences rather than attempting to change or criticize the other person. It is helpful to look for the positives, even in very diverse approaches to the same issue.

ORGANIZED

This trait reflects how organized and determined a person is in their daily life and work. It also reflects persistence in pursuing goals.

High Organized Scores: Those who score high on the organized trait are typically methodical and well organized. They tend to be persistent and reliable, placing a great deal of emphasis on this type of behavior in most areas of their lives. Often quite goal-oriented, they may have well-thought-out plans as they strive to achieve their goals. When out of balance, these individuals can be perceived as pᵣ⸍ ꞩnists, controlling, or overly driven.

ꞩ both individuals score high in organization, they may be ꞩd and goal-oriented. They will likely have the discipline ꞩ a lot of long-term goals as a couple. They value consis-ꞩrliness in many aspects of their life together. Potential drawbacks when both people score high on this dimension include becoming overly driven to achieve their goals and putting tasks before relationships. At times, their desire for consistency and planning will be challenged by unplanned stressful situations or life changes that are beyond their control.

Average Organized Scores: Those in the average range are generally organized. They are likely dependable and goal-oriented but can also be flexible, setting aside work and agendas when necessary. They know how to get organized, but it is not always a high priority. While their home and work space may be somewhat cluttered, they will still know where things are located.

Having this in common can be a positive for couples as they balance tasks, goals, and relationships. They will need to communicate with each other about areas in their life where they need to get more organized and what roles they will each fulfill to maximize their effectiveness as a couple.

Low Organized Scores: Those who score low on organization tend to resist a great deal of structure and are more spontaneous. They may also be less careful, less focused, and more likely to be distracted from tasks. Often easygoing and preferring not to make strict plans, they enjoy settings in which they are not required to conform to strict benchmarks. When out of balance, they can appear careless or disorganized.

When both individuals in a couple score low in organization, they will be very relaxed about plans, and neither person will place much emphasis on details. They are comfortable with a certain level of disorganization and may wonder why some people expend so much energy focusing on minor details. Potential drawbacks when both individuals score low include getting behind on routine tasks such as balancing the checking account, or losing track of things such as the car keys. They need to remember that setting some goals as a couple is important, and they can find ways to compensate for less organization by strategizing in key areas of their lives.

Handling Differences: Couples with different levels of organization will need to communicate openly with each other about their goals, roles, and expectations. It is likely for the tendencies that were once endearing to become annoying, distracting, or even maddening when stressful events come their way. They need to find ways to balance each other out and avoid the extremes of perfectionism versus sloppiness. Potential challenges include different expectations for housekeeping, relationship roles, and long-term goals. Focusing on strengths and allowing the more organized individual to handle necessary details can be helpful, but these couples will need to guard against allowing the highly organized individual to function more like a parent and less like a partner.

PLEASING

This trait reflects how considerate and cooperative a person is in their daily interactions with others.

High Pleasing Scores: High scores suggest a person is trusting, friendly, and cooperative. They value getting along with others, and are considerate and helpful. Optimistic about people, they view others as basically honest, decent, and trustworthy. When out of balance, these individuals may sacrifice their own needs and opinions to please others. In their relationships, these people may find it difficult to ask for what they need.

When both individuals in a couple score high on this dimension, they will likely treat each other with a great deal of respect and consideration. They value cooperation over competition, and heated conflicts may be few and far between. They are at risk, however, of not sharing their true feelings, especially negative emotions. Stuffing opinions and feelings can rob these relationships of deep emotional intimacy. These couples will need to learn to cultivate their assertiveness, realizing that their relationship often moves forward after sharing honestly and resolving conflict.

Average Pleasing Scores: Those with average pleasing scores can be warm and cooperative but occasionally somewhat competitive, stubborn, or assertive. When they feel their rights are violated, these individuals are able to respond and stand up for themselves. They generally know how to get along well with others and are well liked.

When both individuals score in this range, they typically know how to balance consideration for each other with assertiveness and straightforward talk.

Low Pleasing Scores: These individuals tend to be very confident, assertive, and less cooperative. They can often express their anger directly and are sometimes seen as competitive and unfriendly. They are less likely to be taken advantage of and can stand up for themselves. When out of balance, they can appear skeptical, proud, or aggressive. Others can be intimidated by these individuals and find it difficult to develop a close relationship with them.

You may experience high levels of conflict in your partner relationship unless you have learned how to balance your assertiveness.

When both individuals score low on the pleasing trait, they will tend to be more competitive than cooperative. They have the capacity to be assertive and straightforward with each other. Potential drawbacks include conflict, debates, and the tendency to voice opinions rather than actively listen to and support one another. Their communication may be interpreted by their partner as harsh and unforgiving rather than simply assertive. These individuals often need to work on their active listening and conflict resolution skills (see chapters 9 to 11), as listening is often the more difficult part of communicating for them.

Handling Differences: Couples with one partner scoring higher than the other on this dimension may need to practice their communication and conflict resolution skills. The partner scoring higher on this dimension may need to develop his or her ability to honestly express both positive and negative opinions and feelings. In so doing, he or she can allow the more assertive partner the opportunity to truly understand his or her feelings. The partner scoring lower on this dimension will benefit from working to be a good active listener.

EMOTIONALLY STEADY

This trait reflects the tendency to stay relaxed and calm even when faced with stress.

High Emotionally Steady Scores: Those with a high score in this trait tend to be more relaxed and calm, and less prone to distress. They are likely to be calm and emotionally stable even when confronted with stressful situations. In the extreme, they may appear unfeeling or unflappable.

When both partners are emotionally steady, they will remain very calm and collected as they cope with the challenges life presents. They are not prone to much distress as individuals and often handle conflict well as a couple since they are slow to become angry, anxious, or depressed.

Average Emotionally Steady Scores: Average scorers are generally calm and able to cope with stress. Others likely see them as very capable of handling the everyday stressors. When under high levels of stress, they can experience feelings of anxiety, depression, or anger, but are generally emotionally steady and in control of their lives. When both individuals in a couple score in this range, they can use their communication skills, good problem solving, and flexibility to help them navigate stressful times without the extremes of negative emotion. Focusing on what is within one's ability to influence is much more helpful than being overwhelmed by what one cannot control.

Low Emotionally Steady Scores: Those in this range are typically more emotionally sensitive and prone to becoming upset. They often have difficulty handling stress. When faced with challenges, they are prone to experiencing upsetting feelings such as anxiety, anger, or depression. When out of balance, they become emotionally fragile or overly sensitive. Some acquaintances may see these emotional reactions as difficult to handle and will pull away from the relationship, leaving these individuals feeling even more isolated.

When both individuals score in this range, they know what it feels like to be stressed and in a bad mood. They should be able to understand and empathize when their partner is feeling anxious, down, or angry. Their individual moods, however, can impact the couple relationship as well. They need to be mindful of how much anxiety, change, and stress they can each handle. Being understanding listeners and supportive partners during times of stress will maximize your ability to weather life's challenges together.

Handling Differences: When one partner scores higher than the other, the couple may experience occasional challenges. In times of stress, the more emotionally calm partner may need to take control and help the other person feel less frustrated. The one experiencing anxiety, anger, or sadness might wonder why their partner doesn't feel the same way. It is helpful for these couples to remember to work with each other's differences rather than attempting to change or criticize their partner.

THE DOUBLE-EDGED SWORD OF ATTRACTION TO YOUR PARTNER

Sometimes the very thing you were attracted to in the beginning of a relationship begins to annoy or bother you later on.

She married him because he was such an assertive male;
She later disliked that he was such a domineering husband.

He married her because she was so gentle and petite;
He later disliked that she was so weak and helpless.

She married him because he had goals and worked hard;
She later disliked that all he did was work.

He married her because she was so quiet and dependent;
He later disliked that she was so boring and clingy.

She married him because he was the life of the party;
She later disliked that he couldn't enjoy an evening at home.

He married her because she was so neat and organized;
He later disliked that she was so compulsive and controlling.

It is easy to forget the positive aspects of a partner's personality and begin to focus only on the negative aspects of each trait. But try to remember that something in what now annoys you was attractive at some point, perhaps because that trait completes you or blesses you in some way.

It took a while, but Harry and Joan eventually learned to accept and celebrate each other's personality differences. Again Harry appreciated Joan's friendships and how she helped him engage with others socially. Joan discovered value in setting goals in life and pursuing them with her husband. But perhaps most important, both Harry and Joan learned not to take it personally when the other pursued their personal interests. Harry didn't feel guilty when Joan spent time with her friends, and Joan didn't feel neglected when Harry opted to "sit this one out" and stay home. Each learned to give . . . and receive . . . and celebrate. For a time they thought they had married the wrong person, but they discovered that they had married the right person.

You Always Marry the Wrong Person
You didn't really know
what you thought you knew
when you did what you did
and said what you said.
You didn't know what you needed
or what you needed to know
to choose who you chose
so you can't see what you saw.

> **You Always Marry the Right Person**
> Although you didn't really know
> what you thought you knew,
> you really did know
> what you needed to know
> when you did what you did.
> You knew more than you knew,
> you did better than you would
> had you known what you didn't.[4]

PERSONALITY STRENGTHS OF HAPPY VS. UNHAPPY COUPLES

Within the SCOPE personality categories there are specific personality traits that predictably damage couple relationships; the absence of these traits, on the other hand, opens the door to intimacy. Considered together, the following out-of-balance negative personality traits were found in our study to be the single greatest predictor of high- or low-quality relationships for couples creating stepfamilies. Together they predicted with 92 percent accuracy whether couples were happy or not. The presence of these negative traits is not included in your Couple Report, but it must be discussed here because they have the power to destroy closeness and confidence in your relationship.

Couples are much more likely to be unhappy and distressed when one or both partners are moody, critical or negative, controlling, depressed or withdrawn, stubborn, or have a temper. As you can see on the next page, when we compare the percentages of happy and unhappy couples, we see that unhappy couples are between *three* and *seven* times more likely to demonstrate these negative attributes. To be specific, the percentage of unhappy couples reporting that one of the partners has a temper is over four times greater than the percentage of happy couples. Further, the percent of unhappy couples who are emotionally unsteady or moody, critical or negative toward one another, is about four times more. And while 65 percent of all couples in our study reported that stubbornness sometimes is an issue in their relationship (on occasion we're all stubborn!), healthy, vibrant couples are many times more likely than struggling couples to agree that stubbornness is *not* an issue in their relationship.

The differences could not be more stark. Therefore, we highly recommend that you take an honest look in the mirror and take inventory of yourself. Take responsibility for who you are in relation to your partner; who you are really matters.

═══════ Specific Unbalanced Personality Traits ═══════
in Happy and Unhappy Relationships

1. Moodiness is an issue for only a few happy couples (21%), but it's an issue for most unhappy ones (88%).

2. The majority of unhappy couples are critical and negative about some aspects of life (88%); far fewer happy ones are (27%).

3. Control is an issue for 68 percent of unhappy couples, but for only 10 percent of happy ones.

4. In unhappy couples, partners are often concerned that their spouse is depressed, unhappy, or withdrawn (82%); a concern for only 23 percent of happy couples.

5. Stubbornness is an issue for 93 percent of unhappy couples; in contrast it's an issue for only 36 percent of happy couples.

6. Concern for how one partner's temper impacts the relationship is an issue for 71 percent of unhappy couples but for only 16 percent of happy couples.

COUPLE POSITIONING SYSTEM (CPS)

Where are you NOW? (Identify and Discuss Your Results)

a. In what areas are your personalities similar?

- How might the similarities affect your relationship positively?
- Are there any drawbacks to being alike in these areas (e.g., both scoring low on Organization)?

b. Review the following negative personality traits. Which ones might you have a problem with?

- Moodiness. Critical or negative attitude. Controlling. Depressed or withdrawn. Stubborn. Having a Temper.
- How might you help each other rid yourselves of these poisons?

c. Review the Couple Checkup Results.

- In what areas are your personalities different?
- How might the differences impact your relationship, both positively and negatively?
- To what degree have you come to accept your spouse's personality? What still remains difficult to celebrate?
- Do the roles you are expected to fulfill in your relationship match your personality strengths (e.g., Is an individual who scores low on the Organization trait being asked to manage the checkbook)?

Where would you like to be? (Discuss Issues)

a. Choose one personality difference or negative personality trait that you both want to handle better.

b. Share how you each feel about this difference/trait.

c. What would you do differently if you could accept and/or celebrate this difference more often, or what behavior would you implement to decrease the presence of the negative trait?

d. Review the suggestions for dealing with personality differences on the next page. Which could be helpful for you?

═══ Suggestions for Dealing With Personality Differences ═══

1. Don't try to change your partner's personality. It won't work!
2. Be responsible for yourself. The fact that personality traits are generally pervasive throughout life does not give you an excuse not to learn behaviors that will positively contribute to your marriage. For example, in order to serve your spouse, you can learn to pick up after yourself even though a mess in the kitchen or dirty clothes on the floor doesn't bother you.
3. Remember the positive aspects of your partner's personality that attracted you to him or her in the first place.
4. Consider where you may be out of balance in your own personality and behavior. Think of strategies that could bring more balance to your life.
5. Talk with each other about how to use your personality strengths to enhance your relationship.

How do you get there? (Develop Your Action Plan)

a. Brainstorm a list of ways to deal with this issue.

b. Agree on one solution you will try.

c. Decide what you will each do to make the plan work.

d. Review the progress in one week.

Chapter 9

The Vital Importance of Healthy Communication

Healthy communication is the life-blood of every marriage. With it the relationship lives; without it, death awaits.

—Ron L. Deal

What we've got here is a failure to communicate.

—Actor Strother Martin in *Cool Hand Luke*

Actually, couples rarely fail to communicate. Not communicating is impossible since all behavior—verbal and nonverbal—communicates something. For example, the words, "I didn't want to be a stepparent. I married you, not them!" sure communicates a lot. The same message is communicated nonverbally when a stepparent repeatedly walks out of the room or refrains from engaging in dialogue when left alone with her stepson. We are always communicating. The real issue is not whether we communicate, but whether the communication is positive or negative (that is, whether it builds up or puts down) and how the communication takes place.

A common complaint among couples whether in a first or

subsequent marriage is the struggle with communication. Study after study has found that communication and the interactional patterns that surround how we communicate contribute significantly to the health or demise of a relationship. In our study of stepcouple relationships, communication was the number two predictor of couple satisfaction (second only to personality issues, i.e., how well each person liked the personality and mood of the other; see chapter 8). In fact, for couples creating stepfamilies, communication alone accounted for nearly 35 percent of what makes for a happy relationship, and the communication scale in our study can predict with 92 percent accuracy whether couples were satisfied with their relationship. In other words, you better learn how to communicate!

We often tell couples that they cannot learn enough about how to communicate effectively as a couple. This area of marriage has a lifelong learning curve that requires constant attention and the willingness to grow. Just this morning before working on this chapter, my (Ron) wife and I had a disconnect. She was trying to share something with me but my mind was on the day ahead; I missed her message and she felt invalidated and ignored. Even after twenty-one years of marriage, we still have to attend to how and what we communicate. In many ways our communication is better than ever because we've learned so much about each other through the years. And yet, without a certain level of vigilance, miscommunication or negative remarks can easily spoil the day.

Healthy couples know that over the years, personal and marital needs change and, therefore, how communication occurs and the topics they talk about must also change. The good news is that you—with effort from both persons—can learn the skills necessary for open, trusting communication.

STRENGTHS OF HAPPY COUPLES

Our goal is to help you learn from couples who are happy. Experience is undeniably the best teacher. Other people's hindsight can certainly become your foresight. With this principle in mind, let's briefly review the results from our national sample of stepcouples.

First, notably, the percentage of partners in happy couples who feel that their partner understands their feelings is four and a half times more than in unhappy couples. As you'll see in this chapter, the ability to hear your spouse and communicate that you understand them doesn't just happen magically. It takes work and focus.

Second, only 8 percent of couples in satisfying relationships feel that their partner sometimes makes comments that put them down, while 64 percent of partners in struggling relationships do. This finding is consistent with the work of marital researcher Dr. John Gottman, who has reported that critical and contemptuous messages (intentionally insulting one's partner) predict with a high degree of accuracy couples who will divorce.[1] Criticism simply cannot be part of the recurring interaction in your marriage if you expect to build harmony and intimacy. First and foremost this means that each partner must manage their speech and choose words very carefully, because while words cannot break bones, they can kill a marriage.

Another key finding was that strong stepcouples create an environment of safety with each other that allows for open, vulnerable communication. This is evident in that 72 percent of happy couples feel good about how much their spouse shares feelings with them (compared to just 15 percent of unhappy couples). In fact, 83 percent feel positive about how their spouse communicates even in the midst of a problem (compared to just 26 percent of unhappy couples), resulting in the vast majority of happy couples (97 percent) feeling satisfied with how they and their mate talk with each other.

Communication is the lifeblood of any healthy relationship. A decision to grow in this aspect of your life is a significant investment in your marital and family harmony.

Strengths of Happy vs. Unhappy Couples Regarding Communication		
	Percentage in Agreement	
Communication Issue	Happy Couples	Unhappy Couples
1. My partner understands how I feel.	93%	21%
2. My partner makes comments that put me down.	8%	64%
3. I am very satisfied with how my partner and I talk with each other.	97%	45%
4. I feel good about how much my partner shares his/her feelings with me.	72%	15%
5. When we are having a problem, my partner often refuses to talk about it.	17%	74%

STUMBLING BLOCKS TO HEALTHY COMMUNICATION

"A gentle answer turns away wrath, but a harsh word stirs up anger."

Proverbs 15:1

Increasing positive communication in marriage is just one part of improving the relationship. Couples must also decrease their negative communication; they must overcome their stumbling blocks.

A recurring communication exchange between Anita and Michael demonstrates many of the barriers we found in stepcouple relationships. While the topics of conversation below may or may not be familiar to you, notice how they communicate with each other (i.e., the process or flow of their communication).

Anita expected that becoming a stepmother would be an adjustment, but she didn't expect it to be a challenge to her sense of identity. She and Michael had been married about two years when her frustration over her role as a stepparent came to a head. Michael brought two preteen children into the marriage, and Anita had one child in kindergarten. Given that her ex-husband was distant and uninvolved, Anita's role with her daughter as primary disciplinarian and nurturer had always been clear. She relished the role, and her assertive, decisive personality made it easy to be in charge. When she married Michael, who admitted that he was "sometimes soft" on his kids, Anita assumed the role of authority with his children too. Michael and Anita attended one of our seminars for stepfamilies and learned a lot about the stepparent's role in their family. They quickly recognized that much of the conflict they had as a couple and between Anita and Michael's oldest son was related to her premature assertiveness as a parent figure. They mutually agreed that at this point in their family's development, she needed to back off from setting and following through with punishment and allow Michael to be the primary parent in his children's lives. This would become the first step toward healing her relationship with her stepson and earning his trust, which would then allow her to move back into a leadership role. But taking on this new role was difficult for Anita because it went against her personality and forced her to accept the child behavioral standards held by her husband.

"You just don't take enough initiative with your kids," she said. "You've always been too weak with them and they run all over you." Michael countered in defense, "No I'm not. You're just too strict and want to control everything." The criticism and negative assumptions about each other's motives continued to escalate.

Anita raised her voice, hoping to be heard. "I'm not trying to control everything. I just think we should be more structured. And I know why you're not. Your ex-wife threatened to take you back to court years ago and you're still afraid she will. If you make the kids mad, they'll run to her and you'll lose them. But in the meantime, our life is chaos."

"This is not about me," Michael asserted. "This is about you. Ever since we decided to change our parenting you've been depressed and moody. You just can't handle not being in control!"

Is this couple communicating effectively? We would assert, yes. It's effective all right, but it's not healthy. In fact, it's destructive, and if something doesn't change, this couple is headed for disaster. Among other things, this couple has got to stop making assumptions and failing to really listen to each other.

Making Assumptions

One pattern couples fall into that may contribute to feelings of being misunderstood is the tendency for spouses to assume they know each other. While couples are dating, the individuals are often asking each other questions and talking about their life experiences. But the longer two people are together, the more they think they know each other and so neglect to ask questions and continue learning about each other. Assuming you know your partner's thoughts, feelings, and motives can cause you to take each other for granted and jump to conclusions.

Anita assumed that the reason Michael didn't take more initiative with his children was fear that his ex-wife would take custody. This may or may not be part of his concerns, but she didn't slow down to listen to his perspective; she just assumed she knew. In addition, she wasn't considerate of his feelings; she used them as ammunition against him to plead her case. That attitude didn't invite him to share his struggles with her but to defend himself against her. The more he defended himself, the more she dug in her heels, trying to convince him that she was right. He responded with accusations of his own.

Michael accused Anita of wanting control of the home. She may, indeed, struggle with the desire to manage the people in her life in order to bring security to her world, but his assumption and accusation pushed her to defend her actions, not reach out for support from him. Together these communication stumbling blocks create a downward, negative cycle of assumptions, arguing, and defensiveness.

Failing to Listen

The biblical writer James encourages people to "be quick to listen, slow to speak, and slow to become angry" (James 1:19). If there was one communication skill that could be considered paramount for developing and maintaining intimacy, it would be listening. It is possible to hear but not listen. Good listening skills require patience as well as the ability to withhold judgment and spend concentrated energy trying to understand.

In order to relate effectively with anyone, you must learn to listen. This means that you should not be planning your response while they are speaking; you must simply listen with openness, trying to ascertain the meaning of their message. Most people listen while holding firmly to their perspective; that is, they try to make what the other is saying fit their preconceived point of view. When this happens, couples think they have agreement with their spouse but may eventually find that they didn't have agreement after all. To really listen involves withholding your own beliefs.

Effective listening can also be hindered by listening defensively, which is more common if you feel personally attacked by your partner. Your own feelings and beliefs are important, but they can get in the way of objective and effective listening. When Anita criticized Michael, saying that he let his kids run all over him, he immediately defended himself by criticizing in return, "You're just too strict and want to control everything." He felt attacked so he attacked back (a pattern that is sure to speed up the negative emotions in their marriage).

A better response from Michael would be one that demonstrates an important listening skill that minimizes defensiveness and judging: *paraphrasing*. Paraphrasing operates at two levels: (1) restating the speaker's idea by rephrasing it to them; and (2) reflecting the speaker's feelings. Although this approach to giving feedback slows down communication, it minimizes misunderstanding and conflict. The following example demonstrates the two levels of giving feedback by paraphrasing:

Anita: *"You just don't take enough initiative with your kids. You've always been too weak with them and they run all over you."*

Michael (restating the idea—level 1): [Taking a slow deep breath, gathers himself and replies] *"Sounds like you think the kids get the best of me."*

Michael (focusing on feelings—level 2): *"You are very concerned that I'm not managing my children well, and I think you're afraid that they won't learn good self-control."*

When Michael restates Anita's thoughts and ideas as well as her feelings, Anita ends up feeling understood and appreciated. Michael then knows that he is hearing what Anita wants him to hear. Listening non-defensively at that moment would have been a great challenge for Michael (or any of us, for that matter), but the outcome would have been considerably different from what actually happened. A softer answer would have redirected the flow of the conversation away from an attack-defend cycle and toward a more conciliatory share-respond cycle.

We'll say more about this in the section on active listening, but first let's identify your communication style.

WHAT'S YOUR COMMUNICATION STYLE?

There are three common styles of communication in relationships: passive, aggressive, and assertive. The healthiest and most effective style is assertiveness. The following description of each communication style can help you identify both your own and your partner's typical style, and you can better understand how to work toward assertive communication together.

Passive Communication

Passive communication is characterized by an unwillingness to honestly share thoughts, feelings, or desires. It may stem from low self-esteem, and it is typically used to avoid hurting others' feelings or to avoid being criticized. Although it may be done with good intentions in mind ("I didn't want to hurt them," or "I was afraid I'd say the 'wrong' thing"), passive communication generally leaves the other person in the relationship feeling angry, confused, and mistrustful. Passive communication is a barrier to true intimacy within relationships.

Aggressive Communication

Aggressive communication is characterized by blaming and accusatory actions and is often accompanied by language like "You always" or "You never." It is generally used when one person in the relationship is feeling threatened or is having negative feelings and thoughts. When people communicate aggressively, they are often trying to hold other people responsible for their own feelings. Aggressive behavior focuses on the negative characteristics of the person rather than the situation, as we see in the following example. This typically leaves both partners feeling hurt, and it erodes intimacy.

Focus on the person: *"You said you'd get the car tuned up and you didn't. You never do what you say you're going to do."* The recipient of this message is challenged not to become defensive. They also don't know whether to respond to the first message (not getting the car tuned up) or the second (never keeping their promises).

Focus on the situation: *"I am disappointed that you didn't get the car tuned up before our trip. I am really worried about the tires, and the oil needs changing. Do you have time to run it by the shop this morning?"*

Focusing on the situation will create an uncomfortable mood in the relationship, but it also facilitates a more productive communication exchange. It assertively, but respectfully, articulates a genuine concern but avoids unnecessary accusation.

Assertive Communication

Assertive communication allows people to express themselves in a healthy, non-defensive, and non-insistent way. It means asking clearly and directly for what one wants, and being positive and respectful in one's communication. An example of an assertive statement would be, "I would like you to spend more time with the children. Perhaps you can spend one evening alone with them and I can work late at the office." When one partner speaks assertively, it encourages the receiver of the message to also respond positively and assertively.

COMMUNICATION STYLES AND INTIMACY

Communication styles impact relationship style and the level of emotional safety each person feels within the relationship. The Communication Patterns and Intimacy table shows the connection between these factors. For example, the passive couple is typified by not asking for what they want in the relationship, so they usually don't find closeness or connection. The result is a devitalized relationship with a low level of intimacy. When one partner is aggressive and the other is passive, the aggressive partner tends to dominate the relationship, which also results in low levels of intimacy. And when both partners use an aggressive style, their relationship is likely to be conflicted and have low intimacy.

Communication Patterns and Intimacy				
Person A	**Person B**			
Style of Communication		Relation-ship	Who Wins	Intimacy
Passive	**Passive**	Devitalized	Both lose	Low
Passive	**Aggressive**	Dominating	I win, you lose	Low
Aggressive	**Aggressive**	Conflicted	Both lose	Low
Assertive	**Passive**	Frustrated	Both lose	Low
Assertive	**Aggressive**	Confronta-tional	Both lose	Low
Assertive	**Assertive**	Vital/ Growing	Both win	High

In contrast, assertive communication allows both partners to win, increasing the intimacy of the relationship and keeping it growing and alive. But it is important for both individuals to use assertive communication styles. If one partner is assertive and one is passive, the relationship will become frustrating for both individuals, and they will have low intimacy. If one partner is an assertive communicator and the other aggressive, the relationship may be very confrontational, which also results in low intimacy.

IMPROVING COMMUNICATION WITH YOUR PARTNER

A Conversation a Day

Every living thing needs nurturing and attention. If you wanted to plant a tree and have it thrive, you wouldn't simply set the tree in the yard and hope for the best. Instead, you would dig a hole and carefully place the sapling in it. Then you would fill the hole and fertilize and water the tree. And you would carefully monitor its growth, checking for insects and disease.

It is the same with your couple relationship. Your marriage needs attention on a daily basis, which can be as simple as five minutes of meaningful dialogue. We recommend that you set aside five to ten minutes per day and fifteen to thirty minutes on the weekends to share thoughts and feelings about your day, work, stressors, or life together. Here are some things to discuss:

- What you most enjoyed about your day. What you enjoyed least.
- A pleasant surprise you experienced lately or something you are looking forward to.
- A thought that has been on your mind.
- A value you have and how it relates to your life together (e.g., moral values).

- Sharing about friendships or extended family connections.
- Something that has been satisfying about your relationship lately. What you'd like to be different.
- Check in with each other regarding the family calendar and upcoming activities. (If there is a lot to talk about, schedule a specific time to devote to this conversation. Don't whittle away your talk time with "family business" items.)

Couples typically resist discussing negative feelings because they do not want to create problems or arguments. But what really happens when issues are not discussed is the opposite. As with an untended garden, ignored feelings have a weed-like way of taking over or growing up through ever-widening cracks in the relationship. Eventually they may lead to resentment, disinterest, and a lack of desire to repair the relationship. Spouses who wait too long to discuss things that are bothering them gradually become apathetic toward the other. Avoiding issues is very destructive to a relationship.

Self-Disclosure

One way to create intimacy in your relationship is through self-disclosure. Self-disclosure is the revelation of deeply personal information about you, things that most people may not know. By sharing your innermost thoughts and most private experiences, you bring your relationship to a deeper level.

Self-disclosure creates an environment of mutual trust, which benefits both individuals. When you share your thoughts and dreams with someone special, you are, in effect, saying, "I trust you with this information; you matter to me." This invites the other to honor what you've shared and treat it with TLC.

Self-disclosure has a reciprocal effect as well. When we confide in others, they increasingly will confide in us. Studies show that married couples typically share more negative feelings and fewer positive ones. However, those couples who are most happy in marriage share a lot of both positive and negative feelings, making sure that the positive ones outweigh the negative.[2] Self-disclosure connects us; silence, on the other hand, isolates us.

"I" Statements

Both happily married and unhappily married couples experience conflict, but happily married couples have learned how to deal with conflict constructively. In addition to assertive communication, happily married couples use "I" statements often.

An "I" statement is a statement about *your* thoughts or feelings, not the other's. "I" messages are important because they communicate facts without placing blame and are not likely to promote defensiveness in the receiver. This makes it more likely that the other person will understand what it is you're trying to say. In contrast, "You" messages create defensiveness because they sound accusatory. For example, think about how you would respond to the following "I" and "You" statements:

> **"You" statement:** *"You are so inconsiderate to me in front of your friends!"*

> **"I" statement:** *"I feel hurt when you put me down in front of your friends."*

Take a minute to reflect on the impact of each statement. Which is easier to receive and why?

Other "you" statements to avoid include "You always . . ." (e.g., "You're always late") and "You never . . ." (e.g., "You never think about anyone except yourself"). "Always" and "never" are one-dimensional accusatory words that cut down the other person, impelling him or her to deny everything you have said. Before you know it, you're arguing about the one exception to "never," which completely misses the point of the statement in the first place.

Active Listening

"We hear only half of what is said to us, understand only half of that, believe only half of that, and remember only half of that."

Mignon McLaughlin
Journalist

Active listening is the ability to listen accurately and repeat back to the speaker the message you heard. In active listening, the listener verbally feeds back what he or she hears in order to clarify that the message has been accurately received and interpreted. The following is an example of an assertive statement and an active listening response:

Assertive statement: *"I enjoy spending time with you, but I also want to spend more time with my friends. I would like us to find some time to talk about this."*

Active listening: *"I heard you say that you enjoy the time we spend together but that you need more time to be with your friends. You want to plan a time to talk about this."*

Active listening ensures that both the sender and receiver of a message are clearly understood and that there is little room for misinterpretation. Our friend and colleague Gary Smalley refers to this process as "drive-through talking" because it happens at every drive-through restaurant. When you place your order (active statement), the attendant then repeats the order to make sure they heard it correctly (active listening). If they misunderstood your intended order (which they often do), the feedback from the attendant alerts both you and them that a miscommunication has occurred. You can then clarify the order and the attendant again reflects back what they heard. This process continues until both customer and employee reach a shared understanding. The result is a mutually beneficial transaction. When shared understanding occurs in a marriage, the result is closeness, safety, and a sense of connection that feeds future interaction.

Daily Compliments

Giving your partner at least one compliment each day may sound simplistic, but it can have a remarkable effect on your relationship. We often are more inclined to compliment acquaintances or co-workers than our spouses. Giving at least one daily compliment to your partner will help you focus on their strengths; setting your attention to what you appreciate about them can improve your mood and overall outlook about the relationship. It also communicates value for the other person, which invites them to draw close to you. We all enjoy being around people who like us and enjoying being with us.

On the other hand, put-downs and criticism push our spouses away from us. Unhappy stepcouples (64 percent) struggle with putting each other down, while only 8 percent of happy couples do. Instead of making comments to put your partner down, make compliments to boost them up! Think of the two of you as a team. Supporting your partner personally will inevitably benefit both of you. Daily compliments will prevent your relationship from becoming routine and make it more mutually satisfying. Receiving a compliment not only makes you feel good but also makes you feel good about the person giving the compliment.

════ Suggestions for Improving Communication ════

1. Focus on the good in each other.
2. Praise each other often.
3. Take time to listen. Listen to understand, not to judge. After listening, tell your partner what you heard before you share your own ideas.
4. Be assertive (using "I" statements rather than "You" statements). Let your partner know what you want—don't let your needs become a guessing game.
5. Give your relationship the importance and attention you did when you first met.

POSITIVE COMMUNICATION IN PARENTING

In case it's not obvious, let us point out here that all the qualities of effective communication discussed above apply not only to marriage but to parenting. How you talk to children either affirms their value and invites respectful responses or puts them down and pushes them away. This is particularly important for stepparents, who are trying to build a relationship with their stepchild.

Review each of the skills above and think through how you might utilize each skill in your parenting. Don't underestimate the power of encouraging communication in facilitating training, discipline, and punishment with children.

COUPLE POSITIONING SYSTEM (CPS)

Where are you NOW? (Identify and Discuss Your Results)

a. Review the Couple Checkup Individual Results.

- How satisfied were each of you in this area?

b. Review the Couple Checkup Couple Results.

- Was it a Strength or Growth Area?

c. Discuss your Agreement items—these are your strengths.

d. Review the Communication Patterns and Intimacy chart on page 148. Which pattern most accurately describes your marriage today?

e. If you haven't done so already, discuss the use of "I" statements vs. "You" statements from page 151. Which statement is easier to receive? How well do you personally utilize "I" statements when talking with your partner?

Where would you like to be? (Discuss Issues)

a. Review the Discussion Items in your Couple Checkup Report.

b. Choose one issue that you both want to resolve.

c. Share how you each feel about the issue.

d. Rate yourself: How able are you to respond to your partner with non-defensiveness when feeling attacked or threatened?

Circle one: 1   2   3   4   5   6   7

          Defensive   Non-defensive

e. Identify nonverbal behavior that is communicating negative messages to you. Share what you observe happening and the message the behavior communicates to you. Then share what you wish were different.

How do you get there? (Develop Your Action Plan)

a. Brainstorm a list of ways to handle this issue.

b. Agree on one solution you will try.

c. Decide what you will each do to make the plan work.

d. Review the progress in one week.

Chapter 10

Managing the Fires of Conflict

The amount of conflict in a marriage only determines the speed at which the marriage is moving toward greatness or toward destruction. If you want to sit still in your marriage, rule out all conflict. If you want your marriage to crash and burn, let the conflict rage but refuse to learn the skills necessary for managing it. Well-managed conflict is like a stairway that can lead you to higher and higher levels of marital greatness.

—Neil Clark Warren[1]
Author, *The Triumphant Marriage*
Founder, eHarmony.com

A word out of your mouth may seem of no account, but it can accomplish nearly anything—or destroy it! It only takes a spark, remember, to set off a forest fire. A careless or wrongly placed word out of your mouth can do that.

—James 3:5–6
THE MESSAGE
(a Bible paraphrase)

"YOU COULD LEARN A LOT FROM A FOREST FIRE" (SMOKEY BEAR)

One of my (Ron) favorite memories as a child was a family vacation to Yellowstone National Park in Wyoming. I was fascinated by the vast blend of wilderness, mountains, and hot water geysers. But when in 1997 I had the opportunity to take my own children to see Yellowstone, it didn't look quite the same. Nearly one-third of the park lay burnt from several small forest fires that, in 1988, merged into five large complex fires, claiming a full 793,000 acres of trees. Battling the fire required 25,000 fire fighters, as many as nine thousand at one time, and cost U.S. taxpayers $120 million. But how did the fires start and why did they burn out of control? After all, wildfires are common in Yellowstone (an average of twenty-four fires are ignited each year by lightning alone) but rarely burn as many as one hundred acres—combined. So what were the circumstances that led to a significant portion of the park burning in 1988? And more important, what lessons can you learn about managing the fires of marital conflict from the fires of nature?[2]

WHEN DROUGHT LEADS TO WILDFIRE

All relationships go through periods of drought. But severe drought sets up a relationship for the fires of conflict. Despite the fact that Yellowstone National Park experienced wetter-than-average summers from 1982 to 1987 and relatively low fire activity, an overall ten-year pattern of dryness contributed to a significant buildup of forest debris. This would later prove tragic. During the spring of 1988, Yellowstone had above-average rainfall. But by June, the park again experienced a severe drought and the summer months turned out to be the driest in the park's recorded history. Prior to 1988, Yellowstone's wildland fire management plan followed the generally accepted wisdom of allowing naturally ignited fires to put themselves out, which they did quite naturally once the fallen debris in the immediate area had burned. But months of drought combined with a decade of buildup left the park full of debris and ripe for wildfire. In July of 1988 the National Park Service decided to suppress all fires. But the decision came too late. Small fires—which under normal circumstances would have been quite manageable—burst out of control and encompassed more than 99,000 acres of God's wondrous creation within a week.[3]

Sounds like a lot of marriages. Investing in marriage means keeping it "wet" with the refreshing waters of fun, time, and consideration (see chapter 12 on the importance of fun in marriage). Every marriage begins with such efforts and may even have periods of "higher-than-normal rainfall." But stop investing in your marriage and you'll begin to build up debris that is capable of taking a naturally occurring fire—which would normally run its course and dissipate—and turn it into a wildfire than can destroy a relationship.

Healthy stepcouples have conflict, but they make having fun and romance a strategic part of their conflict management plan. Enjoying each other makes times of conflict easier to handle because your attitude toward your partner and the problem is one of collaboration. Having a loving relationship makes you more willing to find ways of resolving conflict. But a relationship plagued by months and years of debris will find that even small fires can rage out of control.

CONFLICT—A USEFUL BURN

Occasional forest fires naturally decrease the level of debris. If ecologists had understood this earlier, the Yellowstone wildfire of 1988 might have been prevented. The conditions leading up to that destructive fire really began in the 1700s when early explorers, who believed that fire suppression was good stewardship, put out all blazes as quickly as possible. In the early twentieth century, park managers continued to view fire as a destructive force, one to be mastered and controlled. But by the 1940s, ecologists began to realize that fire was a primary agent of change in many ecosystems. In other words, they realized it might be useful and healthy for the forest. In the 1950s and 1960s, national parks began to experiment with controlled burns.

Later, in the 1970s, fire management plans allowed lightning-caused fires to burn and reduce fuel accumulations of debris.

Resolving Conflict Healthy and Unhealthy Couples	
Healthy Couples	Unhealthy Couples
• 91% resolve problems. • Over time they weed out unhealthy parts of their relationship by dealing with issues.	• 84% are unable to resolve problems. • By avoiding conflict they stockpile debris in their relationship.
• 95% feel understood during problem discussion. • They have good listening skills and affirm each other.	• 62% don't feel heard by their partner. • The end result is feeling disconnected. • Fears of another relationship breakup become more real.
• 79% are able to keep small disagreements small.	• 83% turn molehills into mountains.
• 74% have unity in the process by which they tackle disagreements.	• 86% can't even agree on how to disagree.
• 90% give serious consideration to disagreement and the need to resolve issues.	• 44% overlook or invalidate the other's concerns. • They don't see the potential hazards of allowing debris to build up.

Couples in healthy marriages understand that the fires of conflict—managed in a constructive manner—are actually useful to the marriage. Years of research have confirmed that conflict helps to weed out the unhealthy or weak aspects of marriage and replace them with a stronger marital alliance and growing sense of security.[4] By contrast, couples who automatically suppress conflict—as did the early explorers of America's forests—discover they inadvertently build up unhealthy, decaying debris in their marriage. And that, in turn, proves deadly later on when a buildup of resentment proves unmanageable. Indeed, a strong predictor of divorce is a couple who habitually avoids conflict.[5]

Conflict in your relationship must be managed, but not completely suppressed. When handled with cooperation, conflict can actually lead to greater levels of intimacy, which was clearly demonstrated in our research (see Resolving Conflict table). Couples in high-quality relationships resolve their differences, demonstrate important listening and understanding skills, and have unity in how they tackle disagreements. In stark contrast, unhappy and dissatisfied couples stockpile the debris in their relationship because they avoid issues, invalidate each other's concerns, don't feel heard, turn small problems into big ones, and can't even agree on how to disagree.

We should add here that a related strength we found in high-quality couple relationships, called couple flexibility (see chapter 5), contributes significantly to their ability to resolve conflict. Flexible couples demonstrate creativity in problem solving, compromise as they deal with each other, and are adaptable—able to change when the situation calls for it. This feeds the couple's ability to find solutions to the complex stepfamily problems that arise.

A woman named Brenda wrote us about her stepfamily of four years; she was about to give up. She had two "ours" babies, ages one and three, and was stepmother to eleven-year-old Luke, who was spoiled by his mother and resentful of Brenda. Brenda wrote about all the influences from Luke's home and her frustration with not having much control. She and her husband disagreed on how to "play the game" with the other household and found themselves divided frequently. We encouraged Brenda and her husband to focus on what they could control and to very intentionally sprinkle their relationship with fun and energy over the next few months. We also talked about searching for compromise and creative solutions to their dilemmas, but most of all, we encouraged Brenda personally to find a way to adapt to her circumstances and accept what she couldn't control. It worked. Six months later Brenda wrote us again, noting that she had found a way to "let go of control" regarding Luke and his mother. This had a powerful paradoxical impact: it empowered her to be more cooperative with her husband when they discussed what they could control. The net result was a more flexible Brenda and a more collaborative marriage.

PRESCRIBED FIRES—UTILIZING CONTROLLED BURNS

In their book *Fighting for Your Marriage,* authors Howard Markman, Scott Stanley, and Susan Blumberg suggest that couples should have regular business meetings to proactively discuss issues or problems in their marriages. This is what we might call a "controlled burn."

One of the positive outcomes of the 1988 Yellowstone forest tragedy was a change in fire management policy and greater awareness of potential fire activity throughout America's national parks. A number of policies were modified, but one significant change opened the door for a more aggressive controlled-burns program in the nation's forests and parks. The unique vegetation in Yellowstone exempted the park from this change, but many forests and national parks increased the number of intentionally set fires on a regular basis to decrease hazardous fire-fuel debris. Interestingly enough, parks implementing this strategy have discovered increased fire-fighter safety, greater structural control when a wildfire does break out, and a greater confidence that natural burns won't explode out of control.

We highly recommend that you too have controlled burns in your marriage. Sitting down weekly (or on some other regular basis) to proactively discuss family decisions, parenting dilemmas, financial concerns, and the status of your stepfamily's growth is a healthy way of reducing the potential of hazardous fires. In addition, we believe doing so will increase "fire-fighter safety" in your marriage (protecting you from becoming trapped by wildfire) and increase confidence in your ability to lead and manage your stepfamily.

Managing the fires of conflict and proactively igniting controlled burns requires skill. It also requires knowledge of what creates the fire or conflict in the first place.

AVOIDING THE FIRE TRIANGLE

Any good fire fighter knows that it takes three things for fire to keep burning: heat, fuel, and oxygen. Remove any of the three and the fire goes out. In couple conflict, *heat* describes an issue over which the couple disagrees; *fuel* is the process of how the couple interacts; and *oxygen* symbolizes each person's negative feelings that drive how they respond to the other. Let's examine each of these.

Heat. Every couple has disagreements. But when disagreements escalate into "issues" there is heat. Ned, for example, loved to buy flowers for his wife, Amy. He enjoyed surprising her with romance and never thought twice about the money. In fact, he'd always heard that all women love flowers and therefore assumed that money was no object when showering his wife with gifts. That's why he couldn't understand why his wife complained every so often. She appreciated his thoughtfulness, but her frugal nature couldn't help but wonder about all the things they could do with the money he spent on flowers. Obviously, Ned and Amy had differing values about money, which brought about heat in their relationship. Ned valued romancing his wife; Amy valued saving for family needs. They had argued about this before, but at this point, no one was listening. And there was more.

Fuel. Even though Amy appreciated Ned's thoughtfulness, the way she responded to him didn't communicate that at all. Once after being presented with a dozen roses, she immediately pointed her finger at Ned and scolded him with her eyes. Ned, feeling unappreciated and confused, jabbed back, accusing her of being too tight with money. As frustrations escalated and each positioned to make their point heard, the two found themselves arguing over a multitude of issues that had nothing to do with the issue at hand—that is, their differing values of spending money. But there was another element of this fire triangle that lay beneath the surface.

Oxygen. Below Ned and Amy's anger were deeper, more menacing emotions. Ned felt hurt by Amy's rejection of his generous gifts, but more important he feared that her disapproval of his gifts meant disapproval of his ability to love and please her. He feared not being enough for Amy. And boy was that a familiar feeling. During his first marriage, Ned's former wife frequently made her disapproval of Ned known. As the marriage deteriorated, she eventually drifted in her commitment and ultimately left the marriage. This left an indelible mark on Ned's heart and created what I called in my book *The Smart Stepfamily,* the Ghost of Marriage Past (also see chapter 6). These ghosts are deep bruises on a person's heart that whenever bumped resurrect overwhelming emotions and often relationally destructive behaviors. Ned's ghost reminded him of how awful rejection is and led him to fear another divorce. The only solution—according to the ghost—was to shower his wife with gifts so that she would feel cherished and return his love. When that didn't work and Amy complained, the ghost activated Ned's fears—leading him to "return fire," hurting her with criticism as he had been hurt. The ghost somehow convinced him that arguing with someone who rejects you can somehow make them accept you (and there's not much chance of that happening). In addition, blaming her for being too tight with money allowed Ned to distance himself from Amy, protecting him from her seeming rejection. *If she can't reach me, then I can't be hurt again,* Ned used to think to himself. Ironically, the oxygen Ned was breathing led him to be angry, reactive, fearful, and distancing—all of which were actually bringing about the very rejection he feared.

PUTTING OUT THE FIRE

In order to stop the fires of conflict from raging in their marriage, Ned and Amy must squelch part of the fire triangle of heat, fuel, and oxygen. Ned, for example, might become a "ghost buster," coming to terms with the difficult bruises from his past that led him to be fearful and then reactive to Amy's values about money. Amy could recognize that when she scolded Ned with her eyes or tone of voice, it made him feel small and childlike. Doing so made it unlikely that Ned would appreciate her need to save money and more likely that she would feel ignored. And both of them could stand to learn a process of resolving conflict that would help them manage the negative emotions that arise from time to time in every couple's relationship. Then, and only then, would ghosts be put to rest and intimacy begin to grow.

In the next chapter we will further explore the skills necessary to successfully manage conflict so that your marriage is one that is climbing the "stairway that can lead you to higher and higher levels of marital greatness."[6] For now, examine the "fire management" attitudes and skills of your relationship; this will pave the way for learning how to squelch the fires of your relationship in the next chapter.

COUPLE POSITIONING SYSTEM (CPS)

Where are you NOW? (Identify and Discuss Your Results)

a. Review the Couple Checkup Individual Results.
- How satisfied were each of you in this area?

b. Review the Couple Checkup Couple Results.
- Was it a Strength or Growth Area?

c. Discuss your Agreement items—these are your strengths.

d. Discuss which of the key "fire management" principles of this chapter already benefit your relationship.
- Keeping your marriage "wet" with the refreshing waters of fun, time, and consideration.
- Believing that conflict is actually useful because it weeds out built-up debris.
- Being flexible as you seek solutions to problems.
- Utilizing "controlled burns" or regular business meetings to discuss problems and make decisions.

e. Identify issues in your fire triangle.
- Heat (topics of disagreement)
- Fuel (unhealthy ways of interacting)
- Oxygen (negative emotions that drive your responses toward the other)

f. What ghosts from previous relationships sometimes haunt you? If necessary, review the Ghost Busting Case Study at the end of chapter 6.

Where would you like to be? (Discuss Issues)

One positive result of the Yellowstone tragedy in 1988 was a change in fire management policy throughout America's national parks. What changes would benefit your relationship?

Talk through the changes, focusing on what you personally need to change.

a. Review the Discussion Items in Your Couple Checkup Report.

b. Choose one issue that you both want to resolve.

c. Share how you each feel about the issue.

How do you get there? (Develop Your Action Plan)

a. Brainstorm a list of ways to handle this issue.

b. Agree on one solution you will try.

c. Decide what you will each do to make the plan work.

d. Review the progress in one week.

Chapter 11

Extinguishing the Fires of Conflict

Happiness is not the absence of conflict, but flows from the ability to cope with it.

—Author Unknown

FUEL: WHEN THE PROBLEM ISN'T THE PROBLEM

The way we handle problems—more than the problems themselves—often can be the problem. In the last chapter we described this as fuel, one of the three components to sustaining a fire. Conflict is a natural and inevitable part of human relationships. How couples deal with anger and conflict is critical to their relationship growth. In fact, the third most important element distinguishing healthy and unhealthy stepcouple relationships was how well they managed conflict.

This chapter will present a specific process for effectively resolving conflicts and, in effect, blocking the fuel of relational fires. But before mapping the process, let's look a bit further into the nature of conflict.

LOVE AND ANGER

"Anger is a brief madness."

Horace (65–8 B.C.)

Just as perceptions about conflict get in the way of empowering your relationship, views of anger also can inhibit intimacy. Keep in mind that, like conflict, anger can be a natural aspect of a close relationship. It may seem strange that we can be polite and considerate to strangers and yet be cruel to our partners, whom we love. But the reality is that, relatively speaking, closer relationships offer more opportunities for anger to arise than casual acquaintances do.

Anger is a destructive emotion that only intensifies conflict. But anger is usually a symptom of some issue within the relationship that needs to be addressed and possibly changed. Feelings of anger must be dealt with carefully and deliberately. Sometimes you have to bite your tongue in a moment of anger, backing off until you feel calmer. As the saying goes, "There are three things that never return: the past, the neglected opportunity, and the spoken word." In a moment of rage, you may say something that can never be taken back and that your partner may never forget.

Once you have separated yourself from the situation and had some time to think through your anger, you will be able to discuss the issue with more clarity. This is important to do. Keep in mind that thinking through anger is very different from suppressing anger. Suppressed anger is dangerous to a relationship because it means that the issue is never resolved. Rather, the issue will simmer beneath the surface, often causing resentment, which can poison the relationship. So instead of concealing your anger or blowing your stack, be intentional about identifying the source of your feelings and then discuss it calmly with your partner.

CONFLICT RESOLUTION SKILLS

Many people simply do not have the skills necessary to resolve conflicts effectively. After all, very few of us were fortunate enough to have had a relationship skills course in school. School may have taught us algebra or chemistry, but we had to learn conflict resolution through trial and error. If we were lucky enough to receive good feedback, we may have learned along the way about ineffective ways of dealing with conflict. Two very common ways that people ineffectively deal with conflict are (1) blaming the other person and (2) bringing up old issues. These provide ample *fuel* for conflict in relationships.

Blaming the other person. Blamers spend a lot of time and energy trying to change other people. They essentially try to hold others responsible for their feelings and see others, rather than themselves, as the problem. But remember this saying: "When you point a finger at someone, there are three fingers pointing back at yourself." In other words, a problem is almost never the fault of only one person; all people involved contribute in some way to the issue.

Feeling anger and assigning blame can become an ineffective and endless cycle. Other people do not cause your problems or serve as the source of your unhappiness. And since the only person you can change and control is yourself, you might as well use the energy wasted on blaming someone to clarify your own thoughts, feelings, and preferences. Ask yourself, "What is the real issue here?" and "What do I want to change?" By focusing on what you desire from the relationship and how that can be achieved, you can learn to use anger effectively.

Bringing up old issues. Couples research tells us that happily married partners engage in discussions about conflict in nondestructive ways.[1] One common but destructive way of dealing with anger and conflict involves bringing up old issues in your relationship. Dredging up past hurts only leads to increased feelings of anger, pain, and defensiveness. And when you feel you have to defend yourself, you are not able to negotiate and solve the real issue at hand. Stay in the present. It is the only place where things are really happening.

DIFFERING CONFLICT RESOLUTION STYLES

Regardless of the issue, most partners tend to repeat the same patterns when they argue. In her book *The Dance of Anger*,[2] Harriet Lerner developed a guide to styles of anger management, labeling these styles *Pursuer, Distancer, Overfunctioner, Underfunctioner,* and *Blamer.*

Pursuers seek to create connections so they can become more intimate and close. Because talking and expressing feelings is important to them, they tend to feel rejected by their partner if the partner wants more space. When the partner or important person in their life withdraws, pursuers will tend to pursue more intensely.

Distancers tend to be emotionally distant. They have difficulty showing vulnerability and dependency. They often manage stress by retreating into their work, and they may terminate a relationship when things become too intense. They are less likely to open up emotionally when they feel they are being pursued.

Underfunctioners typically have several areas in their lives in which they just can't seem to get organized. They tend to become even less organized when under stress. They have difficulty displaying their strong and competent side in intimate relationships.

Overfunctioners are quick to advise and help out when others are having problems. They seem to know what's best for others as well as for themselves, so they are often labeled as "reliable." They often have difficulty showing their vulnerable, underfunctioning side.

Blamers tend to react to stress with emotional intensity and combative behavior. They like to try to change others and put others down in order to make themselves look good.

Couples often fall into patterns of dealing with conflict that do not change. Regardless of what they argue about, they will tend to follow the same pattern. Gaining an awareness of the style each person typically uses is part of the process of developing more constructive ways of resolving issues.

COUPLE EXERCISE
CONFLICT: WHAT'S YOUR STYLE?

Each partner should complete the following scale to discover your conflict resolution style. Rate yourself and your partner on how little (1) or much (10) you behave according to each style. Put a circle around the number that describes you and an X over the number that best describes your partner.

Refer to the previous page for a description of each style.

HIM:

Pursuer	1	2	3	4	5	6	7	8	9	10
Distancer	1	2	3	4	5	6	7	8	9	10
Underfunctioner	1	2	3	4	5	6	7	8	9	10
Overfunctioner	1	2	3	4	5	6	7	8	9	10
Blamer	1	2	3	4	5	6	7	8	9	10

HER:

Pursuer	1	2	3	4	5	6	7	8	9	10
Distancer	1	2	3	4	5	6	7	8	9	10
Underfunctioner	1	2	3	4	5	6	7	8	9	10
Overfunctioner	1	2	3	4	5	6	7	8	9	10
Blamer	1	2	3	4	5	6	7	8	9	10

Share why you rated yourself and your partner the way you did. If you don't agree with your partner's perspective, try to listen without defending or blaming.

COMMON STUMBLING BLOCKS TO CONFLICT RESOLUTION

The first step to managing conflict is not doing what is destructive. Our national survey of over 50,000 couples found that the number one stumbling block to resolving conflict is conflict avoidance: At least one partner in nearly two-thirds (63 percent) of the couples in our study admitted to going out of their way to avoid conflict with their partner. As discussed in chapter 10, this only allows for a buildup of debris in the relationship. Every couple has periods of time when a small buildup occurs in their relationship, but when at least one partner habitually tiptoes around issues with the other, the couple is sure to find their pile of debris growing larger over time. It can then be easily set ablaze by the simplest of issues.

Why do persons avoid conflict? To avoid hurting their partner's feelings (something at least one partner does in 52 percent of all couples) and to end an argument (56 percent of couples). The irony is that while a quick end to an argument reduces tension immediately, many studies demonstrate that it only extends and expands the conflict later on.[3] Again, a small fire properly dealt with now is much better than dousing the fire too soon only to have it rage out of control later.

The second most common stumbling block for couples is one or both partners usually feeling solely responsible for the problems they argue about. The truth is both partners usually have some responsibility for conflict; each contributes something at some point. But resentment is sure to grow if one partner is made to feel the blame most of the time. Marital conflicts become a repeating story of "I win, you lose." Instead of feeling safe to explore the issue at hand, this dynamic sets up a competition where everyone loses in the end.

CONSTRUCTIVE AND DESTRUCTIVE APPROACHES TO CONFLICT RESOLUTION

"Peace cannot be kept by force. It can only be achieved by understanding."

Albert Einstein (1879–1955)

Blocking Fuel: Choosing the Right Approach to Handling Conflict

Over half (52 percent) of all couples creating stepfamilies argue over how they argue. They don't agree on how to disagree, which, of course, creates its own problem while sabotaging resolution of the original problem. The good news is that conflict management is a skill that most people can acquire. Later in this chapter we'll give you a model for containing conflict that, if you both agree to, will give you common ground on which to resolve your differences.

Many components of conflict resolution allow for different approaches, and the approaches used will dramatically affect the outcome and the feelings of the partners involved. Some approaches are constructive, while others are destructive. Let's examine both.

In destructive approaches to conflict resolution, old issues are often brought up. In constructive conflict resolution, the focus is solely on relevant and current issues. When partners argue destructively, they tend to express only negative feelings; in constructive conflict resolution, they share both positive and negative feelings. Destructive quarrelers often share only select information with each other as they try to hold the other partner responsible.

Constructive conflict resolution involves not pointing fingers of blame but sharing the facts of the situation, even if they do not always support an individual's contention. Further, it is emphasized that both people contribute to the problem. Destructive conflict resolution resists change, while constructive approaches encourage change in order to develop new ways of handling problems. And, perhaps most noteworthy, the level of emotional closeness decreases when couples engage in destructive conflict resolution; the result of constructive conflict resolution is often increased intimacy and trust in the relationship.

What makes the constructive approaches to resolving conflict especially effective is an overall posture of humility.

A humble attitude about yourself during conflict means you don't have to defend your every action or attitude; when appropriate, you can take responsibility for what wasn't healthy and ask forgiveness. Humility also facilitates listening and considering the other's opinion or preference without feeling compelled to accommodate or forcefully advance your own opinion. It is a posture of openness and grace, which invites the other to move toward you emotionally. Conflict naturally pushes couples apart, but a spirit of humility directly counteracts that by facilitating softness, gentleness, and self-control—all of which create a safe environment to explore the conflict.

This posture of humility also facilitates flexibility. In chapter 5 we noted that, according to our study, this was a key ingredient of healthy stepcouple relationships. Couple flexibility proved to be the fifth most important quality impacting how couples handled stepfamily issues specifically, as well as what aided overall couple satisfaction in general. It is humility that makes flexibility possible because it leaves each person open to influencing and being influenced by the other. Flexibility, then, is one expression of humility in action. When each partner considers the needs of the other (humility) while bending appropriately to find workable solutions (flexibility), couple conflict is more easily managed. If you are not a naturally flexible person, it is vital that you strive to become so.

The chart Constructive and Destructive Approaches to Conflict Resolution compares the various components of the constructive and destructive approaches. Because the approach you use to resolve conflict will affect the outcome, the more constructive your approach, the greater the possibility of success.

Dealing With Issues and Events

In the book *Fighting for Your Marriage,* Howard Markman and his colleagues discuss the connection of issues and events and the importance of dealing with them separately. Although couples report

Constructive and Destructive Approaches to Conflict Resolution		
Area of Concern	Constructive Approach	Destructive Approach
Issues	Raises and clarifies issues	Brings up old issues
Feelings	Expresses both positive and negative feelings	Expresses only negative feelings
Information	Gives complete and honest information	Offers only select information
Focus	Concentrates on the issue rather than the person	Concentrates on the person rather than the issue
Blame	Accepts mutual blame	Blames the other person for the problem
Perception	Focuses on similarities	Focuses on differences
Change	Facilitates change to prevent stagnation	Minimizes change, increasing conflict
Outcome	Recognizes that both win	Fails to recognize that when one wins and one loses, both lose
Intimacy	Increases intimacy by resolving conflict	Decreases intimacy by escalating conflict
Attitude	Builds trust	Creates suspicion
Overall Posture	Humility	Prideful, self-focused

that major issues in their relationship cause problems (money, communication), they tend to argue frequently about everyday annoyances. This is because, unless they deal constructively with the major issues, related events can easily trigger an angry outburst. These events represent the overall feelings about and attitude toward the bigger picture—the major issues. Dealing with issues rather than events releases some of the power that these issues contain.

A very simple example could be housework. If partners do not share the same expectations for the division of housework and do not work through a solution together, the potential for conflict will remain below the surface, ready to be triggered by an event. Suppose Sarah and Robert have been married for a year. In Sarah's family, housework was divided among family members, while Robert came from a more traditional family in which the mother did most of the housework. During their first year of marriage, Sarah took on the responsibility for the housework. In Sarah's opinion, it simply needed to get done, and because Robert wasn't doing it, she did it.

Lately, however, Sarah has started to resent having to do everything herself. Her work schedule has demanded more of her time, and she finds herself spending her free time cleaning bathrooms and shopping for groceries while Robert plays golf and watches TV. Yet Sarah has not said anything to Robert about her feelings, and he is unaware that there is a problem. One Saturday afternoon, Sarah is putting clothes away when Robert returns from playing golf with friends. Tired and frustrated, Sarah explodes, yelling at Robert about his golf. To Robert, it may seem that Sarah is making too big a deal about his playing golf, but the real issue involves housework, which is not discussed. The biggest mistake Sarah and Robert can make is not to discuss the issue of housework outside of this event. What is bound to happen then is that a similar event will eventually trigger another argument. They need to sit down and talk about their feelings regarding housework, not so much Robert's golf outing, and then discuss solutions.

TEN STEPS FOR RESOLVING COUPLE CONFLICT

"The goal in marriage is not to think alike, but to think together."

Robert C. Dodds
Former official of the National Council of Churches
Psychologist and marriage counselor

When you have issues that are ongoing or recurring, use this 10-step approach to deal with them. Doing so may boost your ability to deal with issues that resist resolution. Focus on one issue at a time, and allow yourselves at least thirty minutes to work through the process.

The following is an example of how a married couple, Jerry and Melissa, used the 10-step procedure to work through an issue.

1. *Set a time and place for discussion.* Jerry and Melissa set aside thirty minutes on Saturday afternoon at two o'clock to share and discuss, focusing on this one specific issue.

2. *Define the problem or issue of disagreement.* The issue they have chosen is a complaint of Jerry's that has caused tension in their relationship several times before. Jerry is upset because he feels that Melissa makes decisions without asking his opinion.

3. *Talk about how each of you contributes to the problem.* Melissa admits to making plans without asking for Jerry's input. Jerry concedes that he is often indecisive and that Melissa is a better decision maker. Still, Jerry often feels as if he has little control over how they spend time as a couple.

4. *List past attempts to resolve the issue that were not successful.* In the past, Melissa has made all the plans because Jerry is slow to act on them. Jerry tries to give input, but it is difficult for him to do that.

5. *Brainstorm ten new ways to resolve the conflict.* For instance, Melissa will not make major decisions without consulting Jerry. Jerry will try to be more assertive in expressing his preferences. They will not make a rush decision. Each night after dinner, Melissa and Jerry will discuss upcoming plans. They will check and recheck with each other about plans. Neither Melissa nor Jerry will make any new plans for the next week.

6. *Discuss and evaluate these possible solutions.* Melissa and Jerry talk about each solution and share with each other what they like and dislike about each one.

7. *Agree on one solution to try.* Melissa and Jerry decide to start

discussing upcoming plans with each other every night after dinner.

8. *Agree on how each of you will work toward this solution.* Melissa agrees not to make any plans without consulting Jerry, and Jerry agrees to practice being assertive by asking about the plans at dinner.

9. *Set up another meeting to discuss your progress.* Melissa and Jerry decide to meet again next Saturday at two o'clock to discuss how they feel the plan is working.

10. *Reward each other as you each contribute toward the solution.* Melissa and Jerry plan to treat themselves to dinner at their favorite restaurant as a reward for their efforts toward resolving this issue.

COUPLE EXERCISE
TEN-STEP PROCEDURE FOR RESOLVING CONFLICT

Use the 10-step model when there is a problem that comes up frequently that you have not been able to resolve. Try it with your partner now. Start with a minor ongoing issue in your relationship.

In step 5, brainstorm at least ten new ways to resolve the issue. Do not judge ideas based on whether they are feasible. Simply come up with as many ideas as possible, even if they may seem farfetched. Brainstorming in this way will allow you to get beyond what you have done in the past that has not worked.

1. Set a time and place for discussion.

_____

2. Define the problem or issue of disagreement.

_____

_____

3. Talk about how each of you contributes to the problem.

_____

_____

_____

4. List past attempts to resolve the issue that were not successful.

_____

_____

_____

5. Brainstorm ten new ways to resolve the conflict.

a. _____   f. _____

b. _____   g. _____

c. _____   h. _____

d. _____   i. _____

e. _____   j. _____

6. Discuss and evaluate these possible solutions.

_____

_____

_____

7. Agree on one solution to try.

_____

_____

_____

8. Agree on how each of you will work toward this solution.

_____

_____

_____

9. Set up another meeting to discuss your progress.

_____

_____

_____

10. Reward each other as you each contribute toward the solution.

_____

_____

_____

SUGGESTIONS FOR IMPROVING YOUR ABILITY TO RESOLVE CONFLICT

1. View conflict as a normal part of a close relationship.
2. Never negotiate in moments of anger. Take some time to compose yourself so that you will be able to rationally discuss the issue.
3. When negotiating, do not bring up past issues.
4. Do not blame each other, but focus on the problem. Remember that everyone involved contributes in some way.
5. Deal directly with issues as they arise. If an issue keeps coming up, use the 10-step model to work through it.
6. Continual conflict that cannot be overcome by these strategies needs specific attention. Seek outside counsel to prevent further erosion of your marriage. See Appendix B on page 243.

COUPLE POSITIONING SYSTEM (CPS)

Where are you NOW? (Identify and Discuss Your Results)

a. Discuss the following. Consider each privately first. Then listen to your spouse's perspective, being sure you fully understand before offering your own.

- Would you label yourself a pursuer, distancer, overfunctioner, underfunctioner, or blamer? Share your thoughts.
- Review the chart of Constructive and Destructive Approaches to Conflict Resolution on page 177. What constructive strengths do you have currently?
- What part of the 10-step model do you utilize currently?

Where would you like to be? (Discuss Issues)

a. Review the Discussion Items in Your Couple Checkup Report.

b. Choose one issue that you both want to resolve.

- By this time, you may have run across a number of topics or issues that need attention. Choose one that is not laden with emotion or hurt.
- Practice using the 10-step model with this issue. Work through the steps slowly and intentionally. Note that doing so may feel rather arbitrary and unproductive. Give yourself time to practice using the skill together.
- Once you have gained confidence in your ability to utilize the 10-step model, move on to discuss other more emotional or difficult issues.

c. In what ways does anger play a role in your conflict?

d. How often do you blame the other person or bring up old issues when arguing?

e. What is happening or what are you feeling when you choose to avoid conflict?

How do you get there? (Develop Your Action Plan)

a. Brainstorm a list of ways to handle this issue.

b. Agree on one solution you will try.

c. Decide what you will each do to make the plan work.

d. Review the progress in one week.

Chapter 12

Leisure:
Maximize Your Fun Factor

Sometimes research surprises you. Of all the factors that highly predict remarriage success, leisure time surprised us.

—David Olson and Ron L. Deal

Couples that pray and play together on a regular basis have a bond that is not easily broken, for both bring about a shared smile.

—Ron L. Deal

Social scientists have long known that enjoyable time spent together fosters a healthy marriage (whether a first or subsequent marriage). But no one—not even we—expected to find in our research that shared leisure time would predict marital satisfaction as much as it did. In fact, shared leisure activity was the number four predictor of a healthy, vitalized remarriage relationship. Why? Because it fosters closeness, friendship, and enjoyable opportunities for you to bond. That's why we've dubbed it the "fun factor" of a great marriage.

THE FUN FACTOR PRIORITY

Healthy couples make time for fun and relaxation with each other. Before marriage this dynamic is quite natural for most couples. In fact, that's how they fall in love with each other. Couples tend to date without the children, and they engage in leisurely activities that facilitate emotional bonding.

Jimir and Alysha met on the tennis court. Every Saturday for a couple months they secretly watched each other practice and play in an intramural country club league. Finally Jimir asked Alysha to play a match, and the rest was history. Eventually they discovered a shared passion for lots of sports, which became a central hub of their time together. Once they married, however, the trick for Jimir and Alysha—and lots of other couples—became maintaining their couple fun in the midst of the complex stepfamily forest.

Carving out time together away from the children when trying to win another person's heart is a sacrifice most individuals and parents are willing to make. But once the marriage is official, there is a natural temptation to shift one's focus back toward the children. While an important balance between marriage and parenting must be sought, focusing on children to the exclusion of the fun activities that brought the couple together is dangerous. Very dangerous. Instead, couples should address their stumbling blocks and intentionally find time together for shared activity.

STUMBLING BLOCKS TO LEISURE TIME

Time. We have all the time in the world, and yet finding time—or is it making time?—to sustain or grow your marriage can be difficult. Jimir and Alysha's struggle to continue finding time on the tennis court was shared by 51 percent of the couples in our study. They wished their partner had more time and energy for shared recreation. The missing fun factor was most notable among those with the poorest quality relationships, who were much more likely to be dissatisfied with their shared leisure time. A full 78 percent wished they had more couple leisure time compared to only 27 percent of highly satisfied couples. The contrast speaks for itself.

Sometimes contrasting ideas of what constitutes a good time are a barrier to shared fun. Nearly one-third of couples don't agree as to what is recreational. One reason for the disagreement relates to the personality differences of partners. Some people are more outgoing and seek social connections, while their partners have less of a need for social situations. This was the case for 47 percent of the couples in our study.

One possible resolution for couples whose ideas of fun or whose personality preferences vary is to find the balance between individual recreation and making sacrifices that seek a common pleasure. Ed and Karen have very different interests. He enjoys golf and restoring his vintage sports car. Karen, on the other hand, would prefer to window-shop every chance she gets. For two years the couple went their separate ways, but eventually they decided that if they were going to find time together, sacrifices would have to be made. For example, last weekend when Karen's kids were at their father's house, Ed decided to go shopping with Karen. Ed's willingness to occasionally join his wife while shopping results in a positive marital exchange that is much appreciated by his wife. Ed doesn't shop because he enjoys it; he does it because it pleases his wife and strengthens their bond. His sacrificial heart brings about a shared smile.

MAXIMIZING THE FUN FACTOR

Strong stepcouples have an active, shared leisure life. When definitions of fun differ, couples like Ed and Karen seek a balance between giving each other the freedom to pursue individual interests and making sacrifices so they can spend time together. Other couples just naturally share the same idea of what's fun, and they pursue it on a regular basis.

Todd and Michelle, like 85 percent of the best relationships in our study, have similar ideas of what is fun or relaxing. Because Todd and Michelle enjoy gardening together, they talk about it frequently and look forward to the next time they can get in the garden. Michelle says getting in her garden with Todd is like taking a mini-vacation from the stresses of daily living. And the anticipation of spending a few hours together extends the shared positive feelings beyond actually being in the garden.

Another strength of healthy couples is not letting individual interests interfere with couple experiences. For 95 percent of strong couples, leisure time together takes precedence over individual interests. This is not to say that healthy couples don't ever have individual interests; 79 percent of them respect each other's unique interests and find a balance between leisure time spent separately and together. But they work to ensure that individual time doesn't come at the expense of the marriage. However, 44 percent of unhealthy couples feel that one or both of the partners is indulging themselves to the detriment of the relationship.

All work and no play may make Jack a dull boy, but that's only the beginning. It makes Jack and Jill's marriage pretty dull too. Fun, friendship, and romance is likely how your relationship got started. Be sure to intentionally keep it an active part of your relationship forever.

GROWING TOGETHER EXERCISE: REDISCOVERING FUN!

The following tips can help you become more intentional with the fun factor in your marriage.

1. Brainstorm a list of the leisure activities you enjoy together. Be sure to mention "biggies" (e.g., a seven-day cruise) and "little ones" (e.g., playing cards after dinner). A healthy marriage has some of both.
   • Now discuss which ones are easiest to implement at this stage of your life.

- Which ones have gotten lost in the stepfamily forest but you'd like to rediscover?

2. List the leisure activities you don't enjoy doing together. It's okay to have an individual interest or activity that you enjoy as long as investing in it doesn't steal time from the marriage. Learning to appreciate your partner's interests is also respectful.

3. Implement a "Protect Our Time Together" policy. Too many couples spoil their date night, for example, by bringing up stressful or difficult issues to discuss. They may have matters that need attention, so they jump on the first opportunity they have away from the kids or office to talk. Unfortunately that quickly sabotages the mood of the evening, and the fun fizzles out of their experience like air out of a popped balloon. Make a deal with each other not to discuss problem issues when recreating. Just enjoy the time together.

COUPLE POSITIONING SYSTEM (CPS)

Where are you NOW? (Identify and Discuss Your Results)

a. Review the Couple Checkup Individual Results.

- How satisfied were each of you in this area?

b. Review the Couple Checkup Couple Results.

- Was it a Strength or Growth Area?

c. Discuss your Agreement items—these are your strengths.

Where would you like to be? (Discuss Issues)

a. Review the Discussion Items in Your Couple Checkup Report.

b. Choose one issue that you both want to resolve.

c. Share how you each feel about the issue.

How do you get there? (Develop Your Action Plan)

a. Brainstorm a list of ways to handle this issue.

b. Agree on one solution you will try.

c. Decide what you will each do to make the plan work.

d. Review the progress in one week.

Chapter 13

Remarriage Finances: Yours, Mine, and Ours?

The challenge for many stepcouples is deciding whether fair will be defined through the lens of pain or hope.

—Ron L. Deal

Talking about the numbers uncovers more than a financial picture. It provides a mirror of who you are and what's happening inside of you.

—Patricia Schiff Estess[1]

HOW MUCH DO YOU VALUE MONEY?

You may have heard that money is one of the topics couples argue about most. Our research shows that the opposite is also true; that is, the level of couple agreement about how to manage money is a significant contributor to the health of the relationship. Managing finances turned out to be the sixth most important factor (out of fourteen) predicting a high-quality couple relationship. Furthermore, the financial elements of strong relationships are, in general, shared by less than one-third of dissatisfied couples.

Since finances are a daily part of our lives as individuals and couples, understanding how they function within our relationships is important. It's just not very easy. Uncovering the many layers of how money impacts relationships is a challenging task. One layer relates to values. What we buy and how much we're willing to spend is determined by what we value. For example, if wearing the latest styles is important to one partner, they will be willing to spend more on clothes than the other. If giving to a local charity or church is considered valuable, then going without one or more dinners out each week is worth the sacrifice. If having a car that "gets you around" is your value, then buying an older, less-expensive, pre-owned car will be your preference. However, if you value a car that will last for years, you will prefer a new or low-mile pre-owned vehicle. Managing money as a couple, then, is in part a convergence of values and preferences. When values differ, preferences compete. Arguments that appear to be about money are often really about values.

Our research found a clear distinction between happy couples and unhappy ones: Highly satisfied couples have common values about the spending and saving of their money. Happy couples showed at least 80 percent agreement on what they would spend their money on, but unhappy couples had less than half that rate of agreement. Likewise, the percentage of happy couples who agree on how much money they should save is nearly three times that of unhappy couples. Value similarities or differences prove once again to be a strong factor in what unites or divides a couple.

WHAT DOES MONEY MEAN TO YOU?

"Money is not the most important thing in the world. Love is. Fortunately, I love money."

Jackie Mason
Comedian and actor

Money is not simply the paper, coin, or plastic used to buy things. It can be a source of status, security, enjoyment, or control. If partners have incompatible attitudes and values about money, purchases are more likely to cause conflict between them. Miriam Arond and Samuel Pauker have identified four common orientations toward money.[2]

Money as status. A person with a status orientation toward money is interested in money as power—as a means of keeping ahead of his or her peers.

Money as security. A person with a security orientation is conservative in spending and focuses on saving.

Money as enjoyment. A person with an enjoyment orientation gets satisfaction from spending, both on others and on himself or herself.

Money as control. A person with a control orientation sees money as a way of maintaining control over her or his life and independence from a partner or other family members.

It is possible for a person to have more than one orientation, but not two conflicting approaches—enjoyment and security for example. It's very important that each of you know your basic orientation to money so that you can be aware of both the strengths and weaknesses of your viewpoint. Building unity as a couple, then, requires that you discuss your differences and how you can play to each other's strengths. Take this short questionnaire before continuing.

FINANCIAL MANAGEMENT EXERCISE:
THE MEANING OF MONEY

Use the following scale to respond to each of the items below:

1	2	3	4	5
Strongly Disagree	Disagree	Undecided	Agree	Strongly Agree

_____ 1. I look up to those people who have been very financially successful.

_____ 2. In making a major purchase, an important consideration is what others will think of my choice.

_____ 3. Having high-quality things reflects well on me.

_____ 4. It is important for me to maintain a lifestyle similar to or better than that of my peers.

_____ 5. Having some money in savings is very important to me.

_____ 6. I would rather have extra money in the bank than some new purchase.

_____ 7. I prefer safe investing with a moderate return versus high-risk investing with potentially high returns.

_____ 8. I feel more content when I know we have enough money for our bills.

_____ 9. I really enjoy shopping and buying new things.

_____ 10. People who have more money have more fun.

_____ 11. I really enjoy spending money on myself and on others.

_____ 12. Money can't buy happiness, but it sure helps.

_____ 13. He or she who controls the purse strings calls the shots.

_____ 14. It would be difficult for me to put all my money into a joint account.

_____ 15. I feel that one of the important benefits of money is the ability to influence others.

_____ 16. I think we each should control the money we earn.

Scoring and interpretation: After taking the quiz, add up your answers to the four questions for each category and record your scores below. Scores for each category can range from 4 to 20, with a high score indicating more agreement with that approach. It is possible to have high or low scores in more than one category. General guidelines for interpreting your scores appear in the box below. Record the interpretation for your score in each category on the scoring chart.

Category	Add Items	Your Score	Interpre-tation of Score		Score	Interpre-tation
Money as status	1–4	_____	_____		17–20	Very high
Money as security	5–8	_____	_____		13–16	High
Money as enjoyment	9–12	_____	_____		9–12	Moderate
Money as control	13–16	_____	_____		4–8	Low

GETTING TO THE HEART OF THE MATTER

When money matters are not about values, they are often about an even deeper layer of relationships: the heart.

"I just don't feel like his partner," said Barbara. "Without a doubt my husband shares his wealth with me and my children—he can be very generous—but that's not the point. Lloyd controls everything and I don't even know how much we have, nor do I contribute to investment decisions. It's like the money is all his, just in case we don't make it. It's been that way from day one when he asked for a prenuptial agreement. How can I feel like his partner when I'm excluded from this part of his life?"

Sometimes conflict over money seems to be about values or power and control, but it is often really about the heart. Barbara had access to all the money she and her children needed, and they were well cared for. However, in her heart, she didn't feel totally accepted by Lloyd or that he was willing to give his entire heart over to her. His unwillingness to let her have some say in his material wealth was, to her, evidence of his struggle (especially since her husband didn't seem to have any problem sharing financial power with his first wife). When asking for more decision-making power regarding their money, what Barbara was really seeking was emotional security and a permanent commitment from her husband. But that can be difficult when money is paired with pain.

WHEN MONEY IS PAIRED WITH PAIN

Money issues in a remarriage are initially paired with pain from the past and can become a pain to the present marriage when negative behavioral patterns go unchanged. Underlying Lloyd's need for a prenuptial agreement and control over their finances was the ghost of marriage past, who haunted him with distrust, insecurity, and the fear of losing control—not only of what he had worked so hard for, but of himself. The only thing that kept him from growing increasingly anxious about his future was staying in control of the money and investments he brought into the marriage. Besides, in his mind, his generosity toward Barbara and her children was more than enough provision; it shouldn't matter to her, he thought, that her name isn't on the house or cars. But it did matter to Barbara—a lot.

Overcoming Fear, Risking Trust, Choosing Commitment

The challenge for many stepcouples is deciding whether *fair* will be defined through the lens of pain or hope. If decisions are being made through the lens of pain, then one or both will choose a path of self-preservation (withholding assets is a way of withholding yourself); if through hope, then a path of risk is likely taken. Given that the risk is extended to children as well, choosing hope demands conscious choice and confidence in the relationship. It requires trust.

In her book *Money Advice for Your Successful Remarriage*, Patricia Schiff Estess reviews five stages of trust first identified by Anita and Edward Metzen.[3]

1. *The Rose-Colored-Glasses Stage.* In those romantic first moments, money talk seems crass or unimportant because the strength of

love will handle everything (naiveté), or there will be no money conflicts (ignorance).

2. *The Don't-Rock-the-Boat Stage.* Feelings of resentment or anger surface. Frequently such thoughts as, *Why should I resent his paying alimony? I knew about it before we got married,* or *I can't stand her cheapness when it comes to gift-giving. I like to give the best,* aren't voiced for fear that any stress would put too much pressure on the fragile new union.

3. *The Lay-It-on-the-Table Stage.* Couples painfully express their concerns to each other, feeling it's okay to be honest; to argue about spending priorities; and to speak candidly about their feelings, frustrations, and fears surrounding finances. A foundation of trust is being laid, albeit roughly.

4. *The Getting-It-Together Stage.* The couple has arrived at a mutually agreed-upon lifestyle and has established an effective method of handling finances and making financial decisions. This doesn't necessarily mean that they've commingled funds, just that they have agreed on contributions—both monetary contributions and contributions of time—and that they have a system in place for managing both jointly owned and separately owned property.

5. *The Achieving-Stability Stage.* The couple really feels in control of finances. Despite the ultimate instability of anyone's financial position, they now feel comfortable adjusting their goals or spending patterns as circumstances require. Their perspectives are integrated. They can handle change.

In addition to integrating their daily and practical financial patterns, did you notice what else is growing beneath the surface? Trust. Each and every stage requires a choice to risk the unknown as the two come closer in heart and mind, but eventually the choice to risk gives birth to confidence and trust. Carla knows what we're talking about.

arly stages of our marriage, we were dogmatic about keep-
'inances separate. We kept telling each other that we were
..., committed to the marriage because we equated commitment
to fidelity. But without realizing it, we held back. Not sexually.
Monetarily. It wasn't until we opened a joint account, about six
years after we were married, that we fully understood what the
word "commitment" meant.[4]

MANAGING MONEY: FINDING A SYSTEM THAT WORKS

A complete guide to managing money within stepfamilies is beyond
the scope of this book. However, we can briefly review the most common systems used by couples. Researchers Marilyn Coleman and
Lawrence Ganong have found that most couples use a one-, two-, or
three-pot system.[5] One-pot couples have joint ownership over all of
their financial accounts (including savings and investments). Two-pot
couples divide monies into his and hers. Sometimes this is reflective
of what each brought into the marriage or the income each produces,
and sometimes it represents the different obligations (e.g., child support to an ex-spouse) and debts each holds. Three-pot couples have
a his, hers, and theirs account from which they pay shared bills and
expenditures. The majority of couples (75 percent) utilize a one-pot
system, and most of them are satisfied with that method. But there is
some indication that two-pot couples, who likely have a higher need for
a sense of independence in the relationship, are also generally satisfied
with how they manage their money. Three-pot couples appear to be
more satisfied with their system than other couples. The system itself
doesn't seem to make a significant difference in the level of couple
satisfaction for one-, two-, or three-pot couples. What does matter is
whether the couple agrees on the system and shares similar values
about spending, saving, and how family members are provided for.
Any system can work, but it has to be agreeable to both. Here are a
few areas of money management that you should agree to.

Adherence to a Budget

How does a couple mutually control their money, rather than having bills and spending control their lives? The answer is in budgeting. Budgeting does not mean cutting back on the things you really want; rather, it is a way to actively decide what you do with your money. It is a conscious, systematic balancing of income and expenses. Or, as one sage put it, it is a way of telling money where you want it to go instead of wondering where it went. Initially, setting a budget takes some time, but you will find it is time well spent. Developing and living within a budget can keep you out of financial trouble as well as decrease stress in your couple relationship.

One good way to create a budget is to keep track of everything you spend money on in a given month. You may be surprised at what you spend money on once you put it down on paper. Both individuals in remarried couples often have managed their own budgets for years and may have different styles or processes for keeping track of expenses and income. Negotiate a system that you can share; be sure to check in with each other after a few months to see if the plan you developed is actually doable given your lifestyle.

Sticking to a budget can be difficult at first. You may need to eliminate impulse buying and really practice being disciplined with your money. Allowing a fixed amount each month for items such as gifts and entertainment makes the experience more pleasurable. Having a definite figure in mind helps you avoid spending more than you can afford. And it is a great feeling to know that you are in control of your money.

Plan for Savings

In creating a budget, you and your partner will have an opportunity to decide how much of your income to save. If you find it difficult to save money, you may want to consider having it taken out of your paycheck as an automatic payroll deduction.

Remember, it is never too late or too early to start saving. And money invested in a safe place at a good interest rate continues to grow at a steady rate. Consider the results of saving just $30 per month at 5% and 10% interest over time.

If you save $1 a day
($1/day for 30 days = $30/month)

Years	5% interest	10% interest
10	$ 4,677	$ 6,195
20	12,381	22,968
30	25,071	68,379
40	45,969	191,301
50	80,391	524,061
60	137,085	1,424,856
70	230,460	3,863,340

Voluntary Simplicity

An increasing number of people choosing to live simply has grown out of the recognition that we have become imprisoned by our lifestyles, material goods, and endless wants. This is sometimes referred to as the "simplicity movement" or "downshifting." Followers actively and consciously choose to reduce their consumption of products, thereby enjoying what they have more, raising its intrinsic value. They spend less time acquiring things and more time acquiring experiences, insight, and relationships. Less clutter in our surroundings frees time and energy away from maintaining those things to spending more time with family, friends, nature, or study.

While the simplicity movement is more philosophical and is not principally derived from the financial need to spend less, saving money could be a positive by-product of such a lifestyle. Couples, individuals, and families can find real satisfaction in using less as a way to contribute less solid waste, but also as a way to be in control of spending. It also offers an approach to be more mindful of your consumer habits, thwarting the negative effects of materialism.

To begin with, be cognizant of your purchases. Ask yourself if they represent a real need. If you determine the purchase is necessary, take some time before actually buying it. Sometimes this will be a few minutes; other times it may be a few days. Either way, this can prevent impulsive purchases. You can always buy it at a later time, but many times you may no longer want or need the item. This is an opportunity with many rewards and few consequences, other than being less expensive and freeing up time to perhaps concentrate more on special people in your lives. If you don't find freedom in having less, you can always go back to purchasing products. Think about it as an experiment with nothing to lose and a lot to gain.

OVERCOMING BARRIERS

Once your values are in line and you have negotiated a system of money management, pay attention to your differing preferences. Here are issues that sometimes hamstring couples.

Spender vs. Saver

Spenders and savers are the classic money personalities. Not surprisingly, saving/spending problems are common among couples because individuals often have different personal preferences of spending and saving. Most partners do not find out until after marriage how different their spending/saving styles are because most (73 percent) don't develop a specific plan for how much money they will spend once married. In fact, over half don't even know what their financial status will be after the wedding (55 percent). Once married, couples with a wide spender/saver gap have more money conflicts.

To better understand the different styles, it helps to visualize a continuum of saving and spending. On one end of the continuum are people who seem to throw money around. These people love to spend money on themselves or on others. They may have personality types that identify more with spenders: spontaneous and disorganized. On the other end are people who compulsively save money. These people may feel anxious about spending money or worry that there won't be enough. The classic saver personality type is conservative and well-organized.

Most people are somewhere in the middle of the continuum and are able to successfully balance their impulses to spend money with their need to save and budget. However, people also tend to lean toward being either spenders or savers. It is these differences in tendencies that can cause trouble or lead to disagreements with each other.

To overcome your spender/saver gap, consider these helpful tips:

- Negotiate a set of financial values that will guide your decisions.

- Commit to letting your financial values determine the amounts you will spend or save. For example, if you value getting out of debt, then the spender will refrain from making more purchases until your debt is completely paid off. If you value a reliable automobile for family trips, then the saver may have to be willing to spend a little more money than he or she would prefer.

- Read a good book on wise financial management practices. Whether you agree on financial values or not, seeking out solid, objective recommendations on money management can further reduce your gap and increase your couple unity. We recommend Dave Ramsey's book *The Total Money Makeover.*

Overuse of Credit and Credit Cards

"Modern man drives a mortgaged car over a bond-financed highway on credit-card gas."

Earl Wilson (1907–1987)

Overspending is another common stumbling block, even if it took place in a previous relationship. Two-thirds of couples in our research have an issue with the debts or settlements of at least one of the partners. Although buying on credit is very convenient, credit cards make it easy to overspend and get into debt. Once in the hole, it is a long climb out. The high interest rates on credit card balances (often double or more the rate on bank loans) can make it difficult for many people to pay back more than the interest and finance charges on their debt. Paying the minimum fee each month may seem easier than paying cash for purchases, but you ultimately end up paying much more for that purchase because of the accumulating interest.

You must realize that by carrying a balance on your credit card, you end up paying two, three, or even four or more times the sticker price for your purchases. Do not let the convenience of a credit card break your financial lives. Blake and Ashley are a young married couple who purchased their first home three years ago. Although they both work, they have not yet added a savings account into their budget. So when their washing machine broke, without much hesitation they bought a new one. Thinking that their new machine would last a long time, they purchased a decent front-loading, energy-efficient model for $649. After taxes it cost them $700, all of which they put on their credit card. If they were to pay just twenty dollars per month on their credit card at the rate of 19.8% interest, it would take them four and a half years until the washing machine was paid for. Worst of all, they would end up paying $1,053 for the washing machine, and this is only including interest, not finance charges or the additional fees that credit card companies often tack on.

So what are their other options? Ideally, they would have begun saving a percentage of their earnings from the time they bought their home in anticipation of these events. If they had started putting just twenty dollars a month, for example, into a home savings account, they would have had the money to pay for the machine up front. But they didn't, so the credit card was the only option they had, right? Actually, no. By simply putting the twenty dollars plus another thirty per month into a savings account, instead of buying the washing machine on credit, Blake and Ashley could afford to pay for it in only 14 months. In the meantime, they may have had to wash at a Laundromat (or perhaps use a relative's machine) once a week, but saving $353 may be well worth a little inconvenience for this couple.

RECOGNIZE THE LIMITATIONS OF MONEY

"The real measure of a man's wealth is how much he'd be worth if he lost all his money."

J. H. Jowett
British Congregational pastor

Many problems people have with money may be socially induced. Unfortunately, in our culture, we tend to define success in financial terms. As a result, many people are engaged in an endless endeavor to accumulate more money, falsely assuming that money will bring them happiness or fulfillment. These people miss the silver lining because they're waiting for, hoping for, or striving for gold.

It is important to take a look at your financial goals and realistically discern what money can and cannot do for you. After all, money is just a tool. There is great wisdom in placing money in its rightful spot on life's list of priorities: way at the bottom. Yes, we need it for provision, but it never buys happiness. And having a lot of money never thirsts our quench for more. Remember, on life's deathbed, no person looks back on their life and finds satisfaction in the stuff they acquired. Instead we prize our relationships, the love we shared, and the contributions we made that last beyond our death. Living today to store up those treasures is worth every material sacrifice way.

What Money Can Buy	What Money Can't Buy
A house	A home
A bed	Sleep
Books	Brains
Food	An appetite
Luxury	Culture
Finery	Beauty
Medicine	Health
Flattery	Respect
Companions	Friends
Amusements	Happiness
Religious pride	Eternity

COUPLE POSITIONING SYSTEM (CPS)

Where are you NOW? (Identify and Discuss Your Results)

a. Review the Couple Checkup Individual Results.
  - How satisfied were each of you in this area?

b. Review the Couple Checkup Couple Results.
  - Was it a Strength or Growth Area?

c. Discuss your Agreement items—these are your strengths.

d. Discuss the following:
  - Identify how pain affects your attitudes about money. Be brave enough to admit this first to yourself, then to your spouse.
  - Before marriage, share openly and thoroughly about your financial past. Hidden matters communicate distrust and imply a posture of withholding. In an environment where at least one spouse has been hurt or grieved by love, withholding is unwise and very risky.

Where would you like to be? (Discuss Issues)

a. Review the Discussion Items in Your Couple Checkup Report.

b. Choose one issue that you both want to resolve.
  - NOTE: Prenuptial agreements, changing inheritance and wills in later life, and deciding on a system of money management are complicated concerns. We suggest you consult an attorney or financial planner in order to explore these questions thoroughly.

c. Share how you each feel about the issue.

How do you get there? (Develop Your Action Plan)

a. Brainstorm a list of ways to handle this issue.

b. Agree on one solution you will try.

c. Decide what you will each do to make the plan work.

d. Review the progress in one week.

Chapter 14

The Sex Connection

Sexuality is the most intimate floor on which the dance of marriage takes place.

—Ron L. Deal

Sex is an important part of marriage. But not that important.

—Barbara Deal
Ron's mother

If you believe the TV ads, sexuality is what you're buying when you get a bottle of shampoo, a pizza, or a breakfast cereal. Given the way we obsess about sexuality and stress its importance in our lives, you'd think sexual intimacy would turn out to be a very important aspect of a highly satisfying relationship. Well, the answer is yes . . . and no.

Our research found that sexuality, including sexual expectations, affection, matters of desire, and how a couple communicates about sexuality, is the seventh most important predictor of a high-quality stepcouple relationship. Without question, sex is part of a healthy relationship.

But while the sexuality scale itself proved to predict with 84 percent accuracy whether couples were happy or unhappy, sexuality only accounted for 13 percent of what contributes to a high-quality relationship. In other words, Ron's mom was right when she told him that sex is an important part of marriage, but not that important. What she meant—and what our research indicated—is that sex contributes to a healthy marriage, but a healthy sexual relationship doesn't necessarily result in a healthy marriage. You better have more in your relational toolbox than just good sex, because sex is just part of the picture.

When sex is going well, it adds excitement to marriage and acts as a regular emotional bonding agent for the couple. The surge in oxytocin in the body that occurs at orgasm stimulates feelings of affection, intimacy, and closeness between partners. Consistent mutual sexual pleasure increases bonding within the relationship. But when affection and sexuality are not functioning well, it can be a considerable drain on the marriage. Dysfunctional or nonexistent sex, say Barry and Emily McCarthy in their book *Couple Sexual Awareness,* contributes to 50 to 70 percent of what drains a marriage.[1]

Keeping a realistic perspective on the role and significance of sex in a marriage is essential. So, again, is sexuality important to the overall health of a marriage? No, from the standpoint that sex in and of itself is not enough to form the foundation for a relationship or sustain it. But yes, it is important, in the sense that it increases intimacy and feelings of closeness while acting as a significant bonding agent for partners; and the absence of sex can lead to a negative drain on a marriage.

The Sexual Connection: Healthy and Unhealthy Couples	
Healthy Couples	Unhealthy Couples
• 97% agree that affection and sexuality is used fairly within the relationship.	• 49% disagree as to how sexuality is used in the relationship and report that affection is sometimes used or refused unfairly.

• 93% agree that they are completely satisfied with the amount of affection their partner gives them.	• 55% are hungry for affection from their partner.
• 89% agree that their level of interest in sex is about the same.	• 53% are concerned that their partner's level of interest is different from theirs.
• 95% are secure in how their partner interprets affection; they aren't afraid of being misinterpreted.	• 38% are reluctant to be affectionate because it is often interpreted as a sexual advance; the meaning of affection is unclear.
• 90% don't have concerns about the previous sexual experiences of their partner.	• 42% have concerns about how their partner's previous sexual experiences will impact their relationship. • They are four times as likely to be concerned about this than happy couples.

SEXUAL CONNECTION AND CLOSENESS

The heart of sexuality is giving and receiving pleasurable touch as an avenue to physical, emotional, and spiritual connection. The meaning of sex is so much more than just whether or not partners experience sexual pleasure. It is about connecting the deepest parts of ourselves to another person, resulting in a spiritual oneness that is unlike any other experience on earth. When a couple's sexual experience reflects this affirming and giving spirit, a powerful connection can result.

A clear pattern emerged in our research of healthy versus unhealthy remarriage couples. Happy couples have a high degree of affection and sexual comfort with each other, including open communication regarding their expectations and issues in the relationship. Unhappy couples, however, report that affection is lacking and the meaning of sex is unclear. There is a clear disconnect in the relationship that is evident in their sexuality.

In addition, a compelling 97 percent of remarriage couples in happy, vibrant relationships (twice as many as unhappy couples) agree that each partner uses sex fairly; it is not a tool to control the relationship. However, nearly half (49 percent) of unhappy couples disagree on how sex is used in the relationship and report that their partner sometimes uses or refuses affection unfairly. They also aren't sure how their affections will be perceived. One-third of unhappy couples (38 percent) disagree about being affectionate given the concern that their partner will interpret it as a sexual advance; only 5 percent of happy couples feel this way. When sex is used to control the relationship or when the meaning of affection is unclear, sexuality quickly becomes not a source of oneness, but a cause of division.

Again, sex is much more than just sexual pleasure. It is a meaningful soul connection that arises when two people share the deepest parts of themselves. At the age of 74, Edna had a strong sense of her sexual self. "I can't jump around the bedroom like I did in my first marriage," she began, "but Charles and I really do enjoy each other sexually." Charles and Edna had recently married, just a few years after the death of their spouses. "I used to think sex was all about positions, orgasms, and how sexy I looked. But then I realized that the most important part of sex is myself. I have to bring *myself* to the experience. And when I do, Charles and I enjoy a tenderness that is incredible." Sex for Edna and Charles is not based on sexual functioning, but on the meaning of their connection. This mature view of sexuality results in a more profound experience of oneness.

THE SEXUAL WINDOW

Sexuality is the most intimate floor on which the dance of marriage takes place. In many ways sex is a comment on the overall nature of the marriage relationship. How a couple engages each other sexually reveals patterns of interaction that reflect other aspects of the couple's life together. For example, outside the bedroom one partner often pursues emotional connection through conversation or shared activity slightly more than the other. The same is often true inside the bedroom. Outside the bedroom, partners may at times find themselves insecure and fearful about being open and vulnerable with their partner; inside the bedroom they may feel insecure about their body type or fear that their partner doesn't want to explore the same sexual positions as they. Sexuality often makes a comment on the relationship in and out of the bedroom.

A good sexual relationship goes hand in hand with a good emotional relationship between partners. Couples who feel safe and secure with each other in most aspects of their relationship have the best physical relationship. For them, sexuality flows from emotional intimacy based on honest communication, trust in each other, a strong friendship, and passionate love. On the other hand, a marriage that is characterized by a lack of trust or that is plagued with destructive conflict is probably not sexually satisfying over time for one or both partners. For many couples, the first step to improving their sexual relationship is to improve the quality of their relationship outside the bedroom. A good sexual relationship cannot be separated from other key dimensions of marriage.

This is especially true for those women for whom sexual desire is a direct outgrowth of the amount of emotional connection they feel with their husband. That's why women tend to find lovemaking very difficult after a conflict; when they feel disconnected with their husband, sex seems out of place. Men, on the other hand, seem to be able to separate their sexuality from emotional connection with their wives. To men, making love doesn't necessarily have to flow from relational intimacy.

How are couples to bridge gaps such as this in their sexual relationship? If sexuality is approached selfishly, couples will likely experience gridlock around these issues. But a humble, flexible attitude that seeks to serve the other partner can help couples build a bridge toward sexual connection. In this case, we recommend that men strive to create an environment of love and affection outside the bedroom so that their wives will find sexual desire more natural within the bedroom. What can women do? Choose, from time to time, to show affection through sexuality even when you don't feel particularly close to your husband outside the bedroom. Sometimes engaging in sex even when you don't first feel the urge to do so can bring about the feelings of emotional connection you long for.

There are many sexual gaps for couples to bridge, even in healthy relationships. Gaps in sexual preference, interest, and gender-based sexual functioning require couples to communicate effectively.

SEXUAL COMMUNICATION

Talking about sexual matters can be very awkward. Most couples in our study (92 percent) had parents who were uncomfortable discussing sexual topics with them. Given that openness with parents in childhood makes sexual conversation later in life more palatable, it is no surprise that one-fourth (24 percent) of all couples in our study reported having a difficult time talking openly with their partner about sexual expectations, and 16 percent were uncomfortable talking about sexual issues. Furthermore, distressed couples have a much harder time than do strong couples talking with each other about sexual issues (27 percent vs. 8 percent respectively) and expectations (40 pecent vs. 12 percent). Yet talking openly about sexual matters is vitally important to being able to overcome stumbling blocks.

Learning to listen to and accommodate each other's sexual preferences, for example, helps to alleviate unnecessary roadblocks in sexual satisfaction. The physiological arousal pattern for men and women, for instance, can be managed if husbands and wives learn to listen to each other. Comedian Jeff Foxworthy observes that women are like diesel engines: They take a while to warm up, but once they do they can run a long, long time. Men, on the other hand, are like bottle rockets: A fiery launch toward the heavens is followed by an explosion and rapid decent toward earth (or in some cases sleep). This mismatched response pattern can lead to great frustration for both partners if men allow their natural arousal time (needing only two to five minutes of active stimulation in intercourse to climax) to control the pace of lovemaking, because about the time the woman's engine is warmed (often needing twenty to thirty minutes of stimulation for orgasm), he is rapidly returning to shutdown mode. If a husband and wife are to overcome this natural difference, they will need to communicate with each other before and during sexual activity so the man can be responsive to the woman's pace of arousal. Engaging in non-intercourse stimulation, for example, is one way for many men to slow the ascent to ejaculation and extend the duration of lovemaking. This increases the likelihood that each partner will experience more satisfaction.

Sexual arousal patterns are just one difference that requires open communication. Couples will have many more over the course of their relationship, making honest, open sharing a much-needed skill for good sex.

SEXUAL SIGNIFICANCE

Luisa's husband pursued her sexually with great passion during the first year of marriage. But that began to change. Ramon began getting up at night and sleeping on the couch. He explained that his back was giving him problems, and sleeping on the couch was actually more comfortable. Luisa, however, feared that it meant his sexual interest in her was diminishing. "It's like he's leaving me on purpose," she shared. "He's been initiating sex less often and I think it's because he is not happy with our sex life." It probably wouldn't surprise you to know that Luisa's first and second husbands both left her for other women and that her ghost was the fear that Ramon would as well. Even though Ramon's behavior had a straightforward explanation, Luisa's fears caused her to judge his motives in a negative way; she believed that his sleeping on the couch was a sign that his desire for her was slipping. Her response in part was to complain about his lack of interest in her both in and out of the bedroom. She accused him of not caring and found herself suspicious of his commitment. This frustrated Ramon tremendously, especially since he reported no change in his care for her. He began to think that her insecurities would make it impossible for him to love her enough. "No matter what I do, it's not enough for her. I fail every time.

And I'm getting tired of being falsely accused." The safety and sexual enthusiasm that once characterized Ramon and Luisa's marriage was draining fast. We'll return to Luisa and Ramon's story in a moment.

Everyone wants to feel sexually significant. We want to believe that our partner is invested in us emotionally and that they are satisfied with us sexually. When one or both of these become suspect, insecurity develops in the relationship.

AFFIRMING AFFECTION

Hugs, a tender touch, and holding hands are all ways to affirm our love for our spouse. A context of affirming affection also paves the way for sexual touch that is focused on pleasure. Again, the difference between happy and unhappy couples in our study was significant. A full 93 percent of strong couples agreed that they were completely satisfied with the amount of affection their partner gave them, but less than half that number of struggling couples reported that level of agreement and satisfaction (45 percent).

Let's return to Luisa and Ramon. Part of the problem for Luisa was that she didn't feel that Ramon was attracted to her. Because Ramon generally thought of sex as the best way to show affection, his frequent departure from the bedroom made intercourse less likely. When Ramon began intentionally trying to be affectionate with his wife outside the bedroom in ways that affirmed her and their relationship, Luisa found it easier not to take his need to sleep on the couch so personally. (We should mention that we highly recommend couples sleep together at night; sleeping in different places for an extended period of time is generally not healthy for the relationship.)

Married couples must intentionally infuse their relationship with a variety of affectionate touch, not just sexual touch. When couples get stuck between the extremes of quick kisses hello and good-bye on one hand, and momentary foreplay on the way to intercourse on the other, connection can be sacrificed. What is often missing is the many playful ways couples can show affection toward each other.

Extended kissing, undressing each other, holding hands during a long walk, gentle massage (feet, hands, back, or face for a particularly sensual caress), lying beside each other on the couch, wrapping your arms around each other during church, and taking showers together (without it having to culminate in intercourse) are all ways that couples can extend the amount of affection given to each other. A healthy dose of non-genital touching is a great complement to the sexual, genital-focused touch every marriage needs. Sex therapist and educator Dr. Michael Sytsma suggests that setting a goal of doubling your normal length of kisses, hugs, and number of sensual touches you and your spouse share can make a dramatic difference in your marriage.[2]

THE POLITICS OF SEXUAL DESIRE

Who wants who more can be a sore topic for couples. The percent of unhealthy couples who are concerned that their partner's sexual interest might be different from their own is five times more than that of healthy couples. When this concern is interpreted by the higher-desire spouse as an indication that their spouse has lower desire—not only for sex, but also for the *relationship*—fear increases, and so do problems in the marriage.

Given her painful rejections in previous relationships, Luisa was quick to see Ramon's decreased effort to pursue her sexually as a sign that he wasn't committed to her and their relationship. This is true in some cases, but Ramon insisted it wasn't the case with him. Luisa's therapist asked her to stop focusing so much on his sexual desire as the only indication of his commitment. She began to notice that Ramon's behavior outside the bedroom evidenced a continued desire to share life with her. He wasn't pulling away as she feared.

Sexual desire is a varied and complex phenomenon that is impacted by a variety of factors. Saying someone's libido is higher than their partner's makes sexual desire sound as if it's simply a matter of interest. In truth, sexual desire is a complex function of emotional, relational, psychological, and biochemical (physical) factors. It can be dampened by trauma early in life or ignited by thinking about sex throughout the day. It can be turned off by bad breath or awakened by a sensual walk on the beach together. It can be diminished by taking an over-the-counter antihistamine or turned on by a random act of kindness from your spouse. Partners should not be quick to judge the reasons for the other's low or high desire, but should weigh carefully the possible explanations.

Remarriage Sex: Tips for Not Getting Caught in the Past

1. **Don't make comparisons in your mind . . . or out loud!** "Why can't you touch me the way John did?" isn't going to breed confidence in your partner. Keep your comparisons to yourself! Nor should you linger on comparisons in your own mind. Doing so keeps you looking back instead of connecting to the moment at hand.

2. **Stay open to new preferences.** Your new spouse's sexual preferences may vary from a previous partner's. Don't think that what worked with a previous partner will work again. Listen to verbal and nonverbal messages telling you your partner's preferences.

3. **Calm your insecurities.** If you were sexually rejected or traumatized in the past, be careful not to let your insecurities or anxiety run ahead of you.

4. **Give yourself time to develop a couple-groove.** Learning how to read each other, when to respond with a specific touch, or what your couple sexual style is will take time. Learn as you go; share what you learn.[3]

5. **Confront your sexual ghosts.** Don't be quick to make negative assumptions about your partner's motivations or behavior. When fearful, try to take small risks to increase your willingness to trust.

6. **Don't ignore sexual problems, and don't overreact.** It's normal for couples to have a sexual complaint of some kind. Don't panic if you encounter difficulty. Talk it through and if necessary, find a sex therapist who can help.

One important explanation for why desire can be different in men and women has to do with how desire is expressed. Traditional definitions of desire center on a longing for sex and the willingness to initiate it (assertive desire). This is more common in men due in part to their higher levels of testosterone (the key hormone responsible for creating sexual "hunger"). But female desire manifests itself as receptivity as well as initiative (referred to as receptive desire).[4] A woman who responds to her husband's invitation for sex can have just as much desire as he. Sometimes men assume that their wives are not sexually interested in them simply because they don't initiate lovemaking. Understanding this key difference can help men refrain from misguided judgments and help women avoid feeling unnecessary guilt over their sexuality.

PREVIOUS SEXUAL EXPERIENCES

A key difference between high-quality relationships and struggling ones repeated throughout this book has to do with the role of fear and its impact on remarriage relationships. This issue also rears its ugly head in the realm of sexuality. When asked about the previous sexual relationships of their partner, 90 percent of healthy couples agree that there is nothing to be worried about. However, in 42 percent of the lowest-quality couples, at least one partner showed concern about their partner's previous sexual experiences. When we looked more closely, the differences between strong and unhealthy couples regarding this aspect of sex were even more apparent. Unhappy couples were somewhat more likely than average couples and significantly more likely than happy couples to report feeling concerns about previous sexual experiences. What seems to be in question is how previous experiences compare to the current couple's sexual relationship or how they might be limiting their sexual fulfillment.

It's vitally important that couples move through this concern so that it doesn't hide below the surface like a malignant cancer, eroding a partner's perceived significance in the relationship or their ability to fully enjoy sex within the marriage. Couples would do well to discuss their concerns, being careful not to compare the current sexual relationship with the past, but to express their desires for how they would like to see the relationship or their confidence in their partner's satisfaction improve. Don't let your fears related to the past go unaddressed or they will limit your intimacy today.

Once Luisa began to trust Ramon's heart again and he continually pursued her with non-sexual affection outside the bedroom, two additional steps helped them move past their frustrations. First, they worked together to create opportunities for lovemaking to occur. Given Ramon's back problems, the couple had to be more intentional and rely less on nighttime spontaneity to present them with opportunities to engage in sex. They began meeting at home for lunch periodically while the kids were at school, and they planned other opportune times to connect sexually.

Second, Luisa began to work on how her fear ghost (see chapter 6) was influencing her to misjudge her husband's heart. She made a list of triggers (behaviors, words, and feelings) that activated her fear and what actions she took when upset. She and Ramon then worked together over time to reduce the ghost's influence on their marriage. Eventually her fears decreased significantly. As their relational and sexual communication increased over time, a strong sexual intimacy developed.

ENHANCING YOUR SEXUAL INTIMACY

Just because sex is a natural function of your body, don't assume you know all you need to know to be sexually proficient. We encourage you to reference one of the many quality books available on sexuality[5] and read it together as a couple. Here are a few suggestions to consider together.

1. Sex is a gift, not a right. A couple cannot have a great sex life if either demands sex or if either believes sex is an obligation. A

great sex life grows when both persons give the best of themselves to the other.[6]

2. Maintain a sense of awe and wonder about sex. The greatest sex organ is your brain. How you think about sex gives it meaning and vitality or makes it ordinary. Remember that every sexual encounter is an opportunity to drink deeply of the one you love. Consider this mystery with every touch and taste.

3. Take responsibility for your own pleasure. Don't assume the other will know when or how to stimulate you. Use assertive communication skills (chapter 9) to share what you enjoy. Trust each other to speak up for your preferences without demanding.

4. Be flexible during lovemaking. While the typical sexual dance you follow as a couple can be familiar and comfortable, do try new things as your bodies and moods change. Take care not to follow a rigid "recipe" for excitement or sexual play. Men, for example, who believe they know their wife's "combination" will find that it frequently changes. Pursue the pleasure of the moment, not some predetermined path to orgasm.

5. Most women need clitoral stimulation to reach orgasm. More than 60 percent of women need direct clitoral stimulation for fifteen minutes or longer to achieve orgasm. Assuming that intercourse alone "should be enough" ignores female physiology. The clitoris is similar to the head of the man's penis and often isn't stimulated during intercourse. It can be helpful (and fun) for a woman to show her husband how she wants her clitoris to be stimulated (lightly or firmly, quickly or slowly, at different times).[7]

6. Be playful. Don't manage yourself like a critical parent. Let yourself go like a playful child.[8]

7. Manage what reduces your sexual desire. When fatigued, for example, women need to get rest and sleep. When stressed, men need to get exercise. Find ways of activating your sexual interests.

8. Eat a variety of "sexual meals." Over time a healthy sexual relationship is like the variety of meals we eat to care for our bodies. Have a healthy diet of each:

- *Appetizers with engaging aroma*—Be affectionate to awaken sexual desires. Small behaviors like complimenting each other, smiling when your spouse enters the room, calling from work with a sensuous message, and having an extended kiss before leaving for work help you smell what's cookin'.
- *Snacks*—Every couple needs quick sexual encounters from time to time ("quickies"). It's not a balanced meal and you can't live for long on them, but they sure fill you up when you need it.
- *Well-Balanced Meals*—Most meals involve the four food groups. Be sure to balance your lovemaking with a variety of types of "food" (engage all five senses). Don't just eat chicken every night.
- *Smorgasbord*—Take turns asking for what you want. Each partner chooses from a list of sexual favorites; take turns being the pleasurer or receiver.[9]
- *Celebration Events*—Most households spend hours planning and cooking Thanksgiving dinner; it's not just a meal, it's an event! On occasion, spend extra time planning a special sexual feast that involves time, money, surprises, and lots of fun.[10]

9. Avoid pornography. It can appear benign, but over time it distorts expectations and makes "normal sex" seem uneventful. Inviting a third party into your marriage is a slow-growing cancer; don't give pornography any place in your marriage.
10. Face sexual problems and get help. Most couples experience some kind of sexual problem at some point in their marriage. One national study estimated that over 80 percent of marriages in the U.S. had experienced a sexual problem.[11] Talking with a therapist might seem awkward, but many effective treatments exist for a variety of issues. When help is needed, seek it out.[12]

COUPLE POSITIONING SYSTEM (CPS)

Where are you NOW? (Identify and Discuss Your Results)

a. Review the Couple Checkup Individual Results.

- How satisfied were each of you in this area?

b. Review the Couple Checkup Couple Results.

- Was it a Strength or Growth Area?

c. Discuss your Agreement items—these are your strengths.

Where would you like to be? (Discuss Issues)

a. Review the Discussion Items in Your Couple Checkup Report.

b. Choose one issue that you both want to resolve.

c. Share how you each feel about the issue.

How do you get there? (Develop Your Action Plan)

a. Brainstorm a list of ways to handle this issue.

b. Agree on one solution you will try.

c. Decide what you will each do to make the plan work.

d. Review the progress in one week.

Chapter 15

Finding Your Spiritual Core

We pray together. We play together.

—Study Participant

Spiritual well-being can be the caring center within each individual that promotes sharing, love, and compassion.

—John DeFrain and David Olson[1]

Ty and Andrea don't just talk about faith—they live it out together. "As often as we can, Ty and I pray together," said Andrea. "It helps us keep God at the center of our daily lives and decisions. It connects us too. I'm not sure how, but I feel closer to him when we enter that intimate time of prayer." Ty and Andrea have found their spiritual core. They not only have personal faith convictions, but they *share* their spiritual values and orient their marital life around them. We believe it is this quality that often distinguishes good marriages from great ones.

SPIRITUAL INTIMACY: FACT OR FICTION?

Despite the fact that 90 percent of Americans pray, 60 percent report that religion is "very important" in their lives, and 70 percent claim membership in a church or synagogue,[2] the notion that spirituality is an important aspect of marriage is growing increasingly controversial in certain circles in America. Separate and apart from the matter of personal faith or opinion, however, the empirical data in support of spirituality being a significant part of intimate marriage is compelling.

The most extensive series of studies on strong families conducted by Nick Stinnett, John DeFrain, and their colleagues has discovered that shared spirituality is one of six qualities that are commonly present in strong families.[3] What is noteworthy about this research is that it spanned twenty-five years and included families from every U.S. state as well as twenty-seven countries around the world. Despite cultural, economic, social, and religious differences between countries and people, spirituality consistently showed itself to be a significant component of happy, stable, growing families.

In addition, a recent examination of studies of religion and the family found that couples who perceive God to be active or reflected in their marital relationship had better marital adjustment, less conflict, more verbal collaboration and less verbal aggression, and fewer stalemates in discussing disagreements.[4] Furthermore, in 2004, Peter Larson and David Olson examined data from a study of 24,671 couples and found that couples with high agreement on spiritual beliefs were more happily married, had significantly better communication, had greater ability to resolve conflict, and felt closer in their relationship than other couples (see graph on page 225).[5]

So what did our study of over 50,000 couples forming stepfamilies reveal? Consistent with these other findings, couples with high shared spirituality tend to have other relationship strengths such as better communication and conflict resolution skills, fewer negative personality traits, more flexibility, and greater emotional closeness. Conversely, those with low agreement on spiritual matters tend to

FINDING YOUR SPIRITUAL CORE

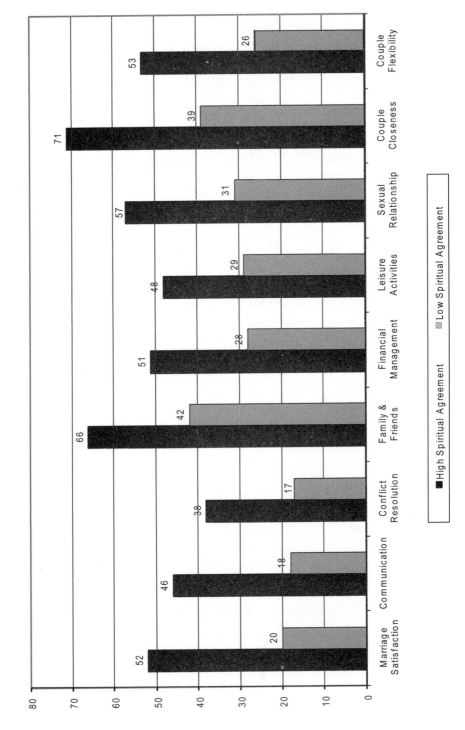

High vs. Low Spiritual Agreement

■ High Spiritual Agreement   ▨ Low Spiritual Agreement

have more problems in these dimensions of their relationships. High shared spirituality in remarrying couples is able to predict with 76 percent accuracy whether they have strong, happy relationships or fragile, unhappy ones. Without question, shared spirituality is a significant contributor to overall marital satisfaction.

THE MYSTERY OF SPIRITUAL ONENESS

"He is no fool who gives what he cannot keep to gain what he cannot lose."

Jim Elliot
Twentieth-century American martyr

"For this reason a man will leave his father and mother and be united to his wife, and they will become one flesh. The man and his wife were both naked, and they felt no shame."

Genesis 2:24–25

Spirituality and faith in God remind us that this world is not all there is. Living for today is, in the end, a foolish striving for things that we cannot keep. But a longing for things eternal not only refocuses our priorities here on earth, but provides purpose, meaning, and a hope for that which cannot be seen. When a couple shares a belief in God and values the same eternal pursuits, a spiritually intimate harmony is created that bonds them together in powerful and mysterious ways.

Notice our emphasis on and repeated use of the words *shared spirituality*. Spirituality is the great unifier for couples, but it also is the great divider. When faith convictions come alongside each other, a couple is bonded as they live life based on those convictions. But when convictions collide, couples are essentially moving through life in opposite directions.

Beth believes money is a tool that could be used for the good of others. A generous person, she felt much convicted to support the work of her local church. Her husband, Brian, who does not share her faith in God, thought she was wasting their hard-earned retirement savings. Frequently they argued about Beth's donations. In the end, Brian agreed not to fuss about church contributions as long as she didn't fuss about his buying beer. What appeared to be an agreement really was a stalemate fueled by a lack of shared spiritual values.

A vast majority of happy couples in our study (90 percent) reported sharing similar spiritual beliefs—one and a half times more than the percentage of unhappy couples—and had discussed the importance of their beliefs at a much higher rate as well. How shared beliefs are lived out also proved important.

Attending church on a regular basis is but one aspect of shared spirituality. Others include praying together, making joint decisions together based on clearly articulated values, and setting behavioral limits and standards for children so as to teach spiritual disciplines. Happy couples know that shared spirituality does not mean problem-free living, as if faith in God is a self-serving path to happiness and personal fulfillment. Rather, vibrant, intimate couples realize that shared spirituality provides direction for life and orients them to that which really matters. It unites them in vision and purpose.

Alex and Lynn were having problems with Alex's teenage daughter, Rachel, from his first marriage. Watching her parents divorce and then getting caught in the middle of their ongoing battles left Rachel feeling raw and hurt. In her teen years she expressed this internal hurt with rebellion and anger. In many respects, Alex and Lynn's life together was going very well. They had two children together who brought them much joy. The complications of Rachel's outbursts and defiant behavior, however, caused them much sadness and pain.

It was faith that kept Alex and Lynn together. They prayed frequently about their situation with Rachel and tried to patiently but persistently parent her through tumultuous times. They consulted with their church's pastoral counselor and over time shared their frustrations with their small fellowship group. The support they found externally from the prayers of others combined with the internal support they found in their faith in God held them up and kept them close together. It was only after Rachel became a young adult and moved out of the home that they saw the fruit of their strivings. Out on her own, Rachel was finally confronted with the undeniable consequences of her actions and decided to change her behavior.

Strong couples like Alex and Lynn are much more likely to be satisfied with how they express their spiritual values; over 50 percent of unhappy couples disagree about how to live out their spiritual values. If your relationship is hamstrung by differing values, it is important that you discuss these differences to prevent the gap from widening over time. Utilize the 10-step model presented in chapter 11 to help guide your dialogue.

HOW DOES SPIRITUALITY HELP A MARRIAGE?

Everyone has faith in something. The only question is in what do you trust? Some trust in their personal ability to perform and accomplish; others in fairness. Some have faith only in what they can see and touch; others in a Creator to whom honor is due. More than ever, the American culture prizes individual attainment, happiness, and rights. To do so within marriage is akin to living life "on my personal throne with you as my servant." Two people who approach each other with that goal will experience many battles for power and control.

Spiritual submission to God helps relationships by teaching partners to consider the needs of others above themselves. Out of reverence for their God, they seek to serve each other. Furthermore, when God is set on his rightful throne, his will dictates how the couple spends their money, their time, and their energy in this world. The result is a coming together in harmony, rather than a competition of power fueled by selfishness. A marriage centered on two people trying to get their needs met by the other creates a spirit of competition. On the other hand, a marriage centered on two people who humble themselves and seek to bring blessing to the other also results in a competition, but it is a competition of kindness.

How does shared spirituality help a marriage? It profoundly orients the marriage around God while teaching the couple the art of loving as he does.

WHAT ARE THE PREREQUISITES TO SHARED SPIRITUALITY?

In his book *The Spiritually Intimate Marriage,* author Donald Harvey notes a number of prerequisites to developing shared spirituality. The first is having a stable, moderately strong marriage. There is something surprisingly deep about sharing life in spiritual harmony. It often requires more of us emotionally than we anticipated; it forces couples to struggle through differing points of faith. And if spirituality is doing its job, it always forces us to confront parts of ourselves that don't measure up to the standards we profess. The process of recognizing this in oneself is hard enough, but confronting parts of one's partner that don't match God's ideal is even more challenging. That's why a basic level of relational health is important as couples work to increase their spiritual intimacy. "Spiritual intimacy goes to the deepest and most vulnerable parts of your soul. To go there together, you need the kind of trust, safety, and security that are born of commitment and respectful handling of issues and problems in your relationship."[6] As you navigate the deeper dimensions of your marriage, it helps if you already trust each other and are able to manage conflict in a healthy manner.

A second prerequisite mentioned by Harvey is the desire to share this part of your life with your partner. Not everyone wants to walk this closely with their spouse. Not everyone wants to be vulnerable with their temptations, struggles, and fears. Not everyone wants to worship with their spouse, and not everyone wants to sacrifice parts of themselves in the service of others. That's why many people profess a faith but don't live one. To deepen your shared spiritual walk, you must honestly ask yourself whether or not you really want to. If not, don't expect to become soul mates.

BECOMING SOUL MATES

The percentage of happy couples in our study reporting agreement in feeling closer to each other because of their spiritual beliefs was twice that of unhappy couples. The majority of couples (60 percent) with poor relationships, on the other hand, found greater distance in their relationship because of differing values. Becoming soul mates is obviously a goal to shoot for. But how?

Begin by finding the willingness to share the deepest parts of yourself with your partner. Openly share your spiritual journey.[7] Our temptations and weaknesses, for example, aren't an aspect most of us want to admit. But they are a part of your personal journey and, therefore, part of your faith journey together. Sharing begins with talking. Then and only then can your mate see inside you and discover how they can pray for you and support you. When this kind of transparency is reciprocated, a stronger bond of trust is achieved, giving each partner greater security in the relationship. Once you find the willingness to share your spiritual journey, complement it with spiritual activity.

A tremendous spiritual activity for many couples is serving together. Finding a way to give back—together—brings blessing to everyone involved. You might work in a local shelter a few hours per month, volunteer to teach children's classes together at church, or work with a ministry over time. All too often couples gravitate toward their own individual interests rather than serving together. Ironically, couples engage in good works but find themselves working apart. Consider, rather, what you might do together.

Other shared spiritual activities include praying together out loud, making decisions about everyday choices by first discussing the spiritual value behind the dilemma, and holding hands while worshiping. It's not necessarily the activity itself that offers a spiritual connection but the effort behind it that makes spirituality real. All of these may feel quite natural to you or very foreign. But each holds promise within the mystery of oneness. Remember, there must be something uncomfortable—while at the same time reassuring—about shared spirituality, or it isn't pulling your relationship to deeper levels of intimacy.

A DEEP SOUL BOND

A follow-up survey of some of our study participants presented them with an open question: What suggestions would you give to other couples in stepfamilies? The highest percentage of responses (24 percent) centered around the protection of the marriage. To our surprise, the second highest group of responses (12 percent) encouraged couples to "keep God in the center of the relationship," to "study the Scriptures together," to "place God first so everything else could fall into place," and to "pray with your children about situations that come along." To these respondents, spirituality has much to offer.

It's amazing to think that many couples go their entire marital lives without having one conversation about things that will outlast them. The spiritual realm of life may be unseen to the naked eye, but it is real. Likewise, the benefits of spirituality to your relationship may not always be readily apparent, but they are very real. But like God, they will never force themselves into your life. They wait . . . on you.

COUPLE POSITIONING SYSTEM (CPS)

Where are you NOW? (Identify and Discuss Your Results)

a. Review the Couple Checkup Individual Results.

- How satisfied were each of you in this area?

b. Review the Couple Checkup Couple Results.

- Was it a Strength or Growth Area?

c. Discuss your Agreement items—these are your strengths.

d. Discuss the following:

- Separate and apart from personal opinions about the importance of faith, in what ways is the research on the importance of spirituality compelling?

- Would you say that spiritual matters unite you or divide you as a couple? Why?

- How might a deeper shared spirituality strengthen your relationship?

- What are some activities in which you might participate in the near future?

Where would you like to be? (Discuss Issues)

a. Review the Discussion Items in Your Couple Checkup Report.

b. Choose one issue that you both want to resolve.

c. Share how you each feel about the issue.

How do you get there? (Develop Your Action Plan)

a. Brainstorm a list of ways to handle this issue.

b. Agree on one solution you will try.

c. Decide what you will each do to make the plan work.

d. Review the progress in one week.

Chapter 16

Can We Get There From Here?

When it comes to growing your relationship, look to the future, but don't live there. Pay more attention to the present.

—Ron L. Deal

Do you remember the joke that starts with someone asking for directions and the drunken man saying, "First you go this way . . . no, that won't work. Try going . . . nope, that won't work either. You know what? You can't get there from here"? Sometimes getting where you want to go is difficult—especially in marriage.

The Couple Positioning System that has been presented in this book is designed to take you from where you are to where you want to go. But don't be surprised if "getting there" doesn't require a little more of you than expected or if you find yourself frustrated along the way. Here are a few stumbling blocks that you may experience, and some thoughts on how to move past them.

STUMBLING TOWARD INTIMACY

"When two people are giving themselves to each other, each finds what they are looking for."

Ron L. Deal

Marriage is not always graceful. Often we find ourselves stumbling toward closeness, maturity, and intimacy. Be patient with yourself and your partner as you try to overcome these common stumbling blocks.

Sometimes One Partner Is More Motivated to Change Than the Other

Change in a relationship usually means work for both partners, but sometimes one partner isn't very motivated or doesn't see the need for change. This can occur for a multitude of reasons. If you are the highly motivated one, don't nag your partner into becoming motivated. It doesn't work. In fact, it usually pushes them further away from change. Focus instead on yourself and changing your part of the relationship dance. Family therapists have long known that if one person changes in a relationship, eventually the relationship changes too. The tango is a two-person dance. If you decide to do the waltz instead, it won't make sense for your spouse to keep doing the tango.

Changing you is not about manipulating your spouse. Change for that reason is still focused on the other; focus on becoming the person you need to be.

Forgetting That the Journey Is Part of the Destination

Following your CPS will inevitably take you through some unforeseen territory. Remember that this journey is part of what creates your destination. In other words, experiencing conflict helps weed out unnecessary parts of your relationship, which in turn improves it.

Struggling to achieve a family identity (a core task for stepfamilies) creates one. As family members wrestle with their place in the family and work through being an "outsider" who is eventually invited to join the "insiders," a family identity is developed—giving adults and children alike a sense of belonging. People who constantly worry about what they have not yet become are blinded to what they have going for them now. When it comes to growing your relationship, look to the future, but don't live there. Pay more attention to the present.

Focusing on Weaknesses Instead of Strengths

In the introduction we encouraged you to build on your strengths. But the temptation to focus on negatives always exists. For example, when asked to examine your Couple Report after each chapter, you may have found yourself obsessing about your disagreement items, wondering how you can fix them. By all means pay attention to disagreement items, but make sure you are rejoicing in your strengths and using them to grow. You'll find you make much better progress.

Choosing Not to Risk

Remarriage without risk will not bring reward. If you have lived through a divorce, the death of a spouse, or the loss of connection with your child's biological parent, you know what pain feels like. The natural result of pain is self-protection. Being emotionally guarded is fine as long as you're not trying to bond with another person; a prerequisite of intimacy is risk.

If you find yourself hamstrung by fear or pain and are unwilling to trust or be vulnerable—to risk—take responsibility for addressing your fear factor. As long as it has its way with you, your relationship will be mediocre at best. Choose risk.

Believing That True Love Shouldn't Have to Sacrifice

Hollywood writes great love stories. But real relationships are not comprised of "soul mates" whose passion for each other never means having to humble themselves, forgive, say they're sorry, or make a personal sacrifice for the other. Marriage is about sacrifice. The paradox, of course, is that when two people are giving themselves to each other, each finds what they are looking for.

Traveling Alone

There is safety in numbers. One of the biggest mistakes you can make is traveling through life by yourself. Our study of over 50,000 couples found that healthy relationships with family and friends—as opposed to troublesome, intrusive, or jealousy-producing relationships with family and friends—predicted with 82 percent accuracy whether couples were healthy and happy or negative and unsatisfied. We highly recommend that you stay close to family and a small group of friends who can support and encourage you along the way. Just don't stay too close.

Yes, you can travel too close to family, especially if the boundary between your life and theirs is not very well defined. Healthy couples maintain relationships with family members and agree on how much influence their extended family should have on their home. Only 10 percent of strong couples disagreed about whether they were too involved or excessively influenced by extended family, but four times that many unhappy couples (40 percent) said family had too much influence on their life. In addition, 45 percent of unhappy couples worried that one or both of their families would cause trouble in their marriage compared to—again—just 10 percent of happy couples. Extended family can be a wonderful support to your life, but you must make sure your boundaries are firm enough that they don't intrude.

Likewise, friendships are important for each of us as long as they don't drain too much time or energy from the marriage. The positive impact is even better when each partner enjoys the other's friends. Over 92 percent of vibrant couples in our study had shared friendships that supported the couple's relationship.

More and more, couples are discovering the benefit of joining a small group of couples who get together to study, grow, and encourage one another. We recommend you do the same. We created a small-group resource to accompany this book so churches can facilitate dynamic groups that encourage and teach healthy relationship skills to couples. If your church doesn't have a program like this, perhaps you can suggest that they begin one with this resource. Visit *www.SuccessfulStepfamilies.com* for information on our group study materials.

Not Following Through and Not Holding On

The CPS process throughout the book has invited you to discuss issues and develop an action plan for change. But sometimes even the best of us don't follow through on the plan. A missed assignment every once in a while is understandable, but if you have been MIA repeatedly, it's time to step up to the plate. Otherwise, what you are saying with your lack of action is that you are comfortable with the way things are. If that's the way you feel, at least acknowledge it out loud to your partner. If not, then it's time to get busy. Even if you don't see how following through will help, just do it.

If you're trying to find motivation but just can't, take a good look at whether or not you've lost hope. Holding on to hope is the key to finding the personal motivation you need to change, grow, and risk. Once someone gives up hope, there's not much anyone can do to help them improve their relationship.

If you've lost hope in yourself and your partner, find it in the One who gives strength to the weary. God is able to bring change to our lives even when we can't imagine how it will come. Put into action the wisdom of healthy relationships, and trust God to handle the rest.

CAN *YOU* GET THERE?

Yes, you can. It might take a little more time and a little more personal growth than you expected, but we believe the vast majority of couples can mature their relationship and deepen their intimacy. One of the reasons couples divorce is because they are stubbornly selfish and unwilling to grow. May we suggest that you be *stubbornly persistent* in developing yourself as a person and growing your marriage? Determination will serve you well if you let it.

Finally, let us congratulate you on completing your Couple Checkup. Yes, your car needs its oil changed, your teeth need an exam on a regular basis, your body needs a physical once a year, and your relationship needs—and deserves—a checkup. How else will you know where you are, where you need to go, and how to get there?

Put a reminder on your calendar for one year from now to take the Couple Checkup again. By then much will have changed, but the journey toward intimacy will continue.

National Sample of Couples and Remarriage

The National Sample consisted of 50,575 premarital couples who took the PREPARE-MC inventory between 2000 and 2007. The couples took the inventory as part of couples' enrichment, couples' therapy, or premarital counseling. It was administered by a professional counselor or clergyperson who had been trained to use the PREPARE/ENRICH Inventories. (The online Couple Checkup is a reformatted version of the PREPARE-MC inventory used in our study.)

From this total sample of 50,575 premarital couples, the most happy couples (n=15,056) and the most unhappy couples (n=15,433) were separated for much of the analysis. The level of marital happiness was assessed based on the Positive Couple Agreement (PCA) scores from each of the scales. Couples grouped into the "happy" subgroup had PCA scores on PREPARE-MC of 75% or higher. The "unhappy" subgroup had PCA scores on PREPARE-MC of 55% or lower. Couples with PCA scores between 56 to 74% were excluded from the happy or unhappy group since, typically, one partner was considerably more happy than the other.

STATES REPRESENTED IN SAMPLE

The National Sample represented all fifty states, with the largest percentages coming from Minnesota (11.2%), California (8%), Michigan (6.9%), and Texas (6.3%). A significant percentage also came from Wisconsin (5.3%), Illinois (4.6%), Ohio (3.7%), Florida (3.7%), Pennsylvania (3.2%), and Washington (3.2%). Eight states had between 2 to 3% of the sample: Colorado, Georgia, Iowa, Indiana, Kansas, Missouri, Oregon, and Virginia. Eleven more states represented between 1 to 2% of the sample: Arizona, Kentucky, Maryland, North Carolina, North Dakota, Nebraska, New Jersey, New York, Oklahoma, South Dakota, and Tennessee. The remaining states had less than 1% of the total sample.

AGE DISTRIBUTION

Almost two-thirds (32%) of the sample were 41 years of age or older, while 15% were between 21 and 25 years of age, 17% were between 26 and 30 years of age, and 18% were between 31 and 35 years of age. Another 17% were between 36 and 40 years of age and only 1% of the sample was less than twenty years of age.

YEARS KNOWN PARTNER

Eighteen percent of survey participants reported knowing their partner for less than one year, one-third (35%) reported knowing their partner for between one and two years, 22% reported knowing their partner for between three and four years, and about a quarter (26%) reported knowing their partner for five or more years.

EDUCATION COMPLETED

For the total sample, about one-fifth (24.3% of males and 19.1% of females) had finished high school or had some high school education. About 40% (40.7% of males and 43.8% of females) had some college or technical college, while 19.6% of males and 20.5% of females had a four-year college degree. Over one-sixth (15.5% of males and 16.6% of females) had a graduate or professional degree.

EMPLOYMENT

The majority (88.1% of males and 72.3% of females) of the sample were employed full time, while 3% of males and 12.6% of females had part-time jobs. Another 5.3% of males and 4.5% of females had full- and part-time jobs. Unemployed persons made up 3.6% of males and 10.6% of females of the total sample.

Annual Income	Males	Females
$0–$9,999	2.8%	13.1%
$10K–$19,999	7.7%	17.5%
$20K–$29,999	17.8%	23.8%
$30K–$39,999	20.3%	18.6%
$40K–$49,999	16.0%	11.3%
$50K–$74,999	19.9%	10.6%
$75K–$99,999	7.2%	2.9%
$100K or more	8.4%	2.2%

RELIGIOUS AFFILIATION

In terms of religious affiliation, the largest percentage of the survey participants (44%) were Protestant. Another large percentage (39%) identified with "other"—a range of diverse faiths. Sixteen percent were Catholic and 1% were Jewish.

ETHNIC BACKGROUND

The vast majority of the National Sample was Caucasian (87%), while 5% was African American, 3% was Hispanic/Latino, 3% was "other," 2% was mixed ethnicity, and 1% was Asian American.

CURRENT LIVING ARRANGEMENT

Couples in our study took the PREPARE-MC in preparation for marriage. Almost half (49%) of the sample reported living with their partner; 29% reported living alone; 15% reported living with others, and 7% reported living with their parents.

RESIDENCE

Eighteen percent of the sample lived in a rural area; 27% lived in the suburbs; 31% lived in a small city, and 24% lived in a large city.

MARITAL STATUS

A majority (59%) of the individuals in our sample were divorced; 37% were never married, and 4% were widowed.

TOTAL NUMBER OF CHILDREN BETWEEN BOTH PARTNERS

While only 8% had one child, about a quarter (27%) had two children, another quarter (27%) had three children, 17% had four children, and one-fifth (20%) had five or more children.

If You Have
Ongoing Relationship Problems:

Finding Help When You Need It

Some relationship problems are like having a cold. Your nose runs or is stopped up, your head aches, and your body aches. For a time you feel horrible. The good news is that after a few days, the cold is gone and you're pretty much back to business.

Some relationship problems, however, are more like a sinus infection. At first a sinus infection looks and feels very similar to the common cold, but it doesn't go away. In fact, it gets worse as time passes. That's when you know it's time to see a doctor.

Every couple has relationship problems to a degree. But when problems persist and don't go away over time, it's time to see a doctor—a therapist, that is. Even if only one of you thinks the problem is significant enough to seek help, we encourage you to do just that—find help.

There are many types of counselors, marriage therapists, psychologists, and marriage therapy intensives available throughout the country. Finding one you trust can be difficult. Here are some options to consider and organizations that can help. Before blindly looking for a counselor in your city phone book, contact a local professional or your church and ask for a referral.

American Association of Christian Counselors
"Find a Counselor" search available at *www.aacc.net*.
Phone: 1-800-526-8673

American Association for Marriage & Family Therapy
Therapist Locator service available at *www.aamft.org*.
Phone: 703-838-9808

Couple Checkup and the PREPARE-ENRICH Program, Dr. David Olson, Founder
"Find a Facilitator" feature helps you find a counselor or clergy person trained in the PREPARE-ENRICH Program, which is the comprehensive version of the Couple Checkup program.
www.PREPARE-ENRICH.com
www.couplecheckup.com

National Registry of Marriage Friendly Therapists, Dr. William Doherty, Co-Founder
Find a listing of pro-commitment therapists who are trained specifically in marital therapy at *www.marriagefriendlytherapists.com*.

Successful Stepfamilies, Ron L. Deal, President
Offers online articles, resources, training for educators and church leaders, phone coaching, and therapy intensives for couples in crisis.
"Building a Successful Stepfamily" conferences held throughout the country.
www.SuccessfulStepfamilies.com
Phone: 806-356-7701

Unfortunately, not all therapists have training in the treatment of remarriage and stepfamilies. We suggest you ask these questions when calling a therapist before making an appointment.

> *What specific training have you had in marital therapy? What portion of your academic training was in marriage and family therapy?*
>
> *What specific training have you had in remarriage or step-family therapy?*
>
> *How might you treat a stepfamily situation differently from a biological family?*
>
> *Give me an example of advice you give remarried couples or stepfamilies that is different from advice you give other families or couples.*
>
> *What books would you recommend on the subject?*

If a therapist is not able to answer these questions quickly and decisively, find someone else.

Notes

CHAPTER 1

1. All names and recognizable details have been changed throughout this book to protect the privacy of couples.

CHAPTER 2

1. R. Gilbert, *Bits & Pieces* (Fairfield, NJ: Economics Press, 1997), 18–19.

CHAPTER 3

1. This statistic is generally accepted by those who conduct qualitative marital research; based on our research and experience, we agree.

2. U.S. Bureau of the Census. *Statistical Abstract of the United States*, 122nd ed. Washington, DC: U.S. Government Printing Office, 2006.

3. E. M. Hetherington and J. Kelly, *For Better or For Worse: Divorce Reconsidered* (New York: W. W. Norton & Company, 2002).

4. See also James Bray, *Stepfamilies: Love, Marriage, and Parenting in the First Decade* (New York: Broadway Books, 1988).

5. Patricia Papernow, *Becoming a Stepfamily: Patterns of Development in Remarried Families* (New York: Gardner Press, 1993).

CHAPTER 4

1. D. H. Olson, *PREPARE/ENRICH Program: Version 2000*

(Minneapolis: Life Innovations, Inc., 2000) and D. H. Olson and B. J. Fowers, "Five types of marriages: An empirical typology based on ENRICH." *The Family Journal: Counseling and Therapy for Couples & Families* 1, no. 3 (1993), 196–207.

2. B. J. Fowers, K. H. Montel, and D. H. Olson, "Predicting marital success for premarital couple types based on PREPARE." *Journal of Marital and Family Therapy*, 22, no. 1 (1996), 103–119.

3. Ibid.

4. Ibid.

5. Ibid.

6. Ibid.

7. Ibid.

Chapter 5

1. John M. Gottman, *Why Marriages Succeed or Fail: And How You Can Make Yours Last* (New York: Simon & Schuster, 1995).

Chapter 6

1. The stepfamily issues scale alone was able to predict with 94 percent accuracy couples who had high-quality relationships versus those with low-quality relationships. How couples handle stepfamily issues is very important to the success of their couple relationship.

2. S. Browning, "Why Didn't Our Two Years of Dating Make the Remarriage Easier?" *Stepfamilies, www.saafamilies.org* (Summer, 2000), 6.

3. E. M. Hetherington and J. Kelly, *For Better or For Worse: Divorce Reconsidered* (New York: W. W. Norton & Company, 2002).

4. In our self-report study the specific number was 49 percent.

5. As reported by David Olson and Amy Olson-Sigg, "Overview of Cohabitation Research: For Use with PREPARE-CC" (Minneapolis: Life Innovations, Inc., 2007).

6. S. Kennedy and L. Bumpass, "Cohabitation and children's living arrangements: New estimates from the United States" (unpublished manuscript, University of Wisconsin, Center for Demography, 2007). NOTE: About half of cohabiting couples marry or break up after two years of cohabitation.

NOTES

7. J. G. Bahmann, L. D. Johnston, and P. M. O'Malley, "Monitoring the Future: Questionnaire responses from the nation's high school seniors, 2000" (Ann Arbor, MI: Institute for Social Research, University of Michigan, 2000).

8. David Olson and Amy Olson-Sigg.

9. As reported in Ibid.

10. L. Waite and M. Gallagher, *The Case for Marriage: Why Married People Are Happier, Healthier and Better Off Financially* (New York: Doubleday, 2000).

11. Ibid.

12. Ibid.

13. Ibid.

14. J. S. Barber and W. G. Axinn, "Living arrangements and family formation attitudes in early adulthood," *Journal of Marriage and the Family,* Vol. 59 (1997), 595–611.

15. D. Olson, "Comparative analysis of couple living arrangements before marriage" (Minneapolis: Life Innovations, Inc., 2001).

16. D. Popenoe and B. Whitehead, "Should we live together? What young adults need to know about cohabitation before marriage" (New Brunswick, NJ: The National Marriage Project, 1999).

CHAPTER 7

1. U.S. Bureau of the Census. *Statistical Abstract of the United States,* 122nd ed. Washington, DC: U.S. Government Printing Office, 2006.

2. Author and speaker Josh McDowell is credited with first articulating this parenting principle.

3. Dr. Susan Gamach, "Parental status: A new construct describing adolescent perceptions of stepfathers" (PhD diss., University of British Columbia, 2000).

4. John and Emily Visher, *How to Win as a Stepfamily,* 2nd ed. (New York: Brunner/Mazel, 1991).

5. James Bray, *Stepfamilies: Love, Marriage, and Parenting in the First Decade* (New York: Broadway Books, 1998).

6. John and Emily Visher, 110–112.

7. Diana Baumrind, *Child Maltreatment and Optimal Caregiving in Social Contexts* (New York: Garland, 1995).

8. E. F. Kouneski, "Fatherhood Today" (unpublished article, Family Social Science, University of Minnesota, 1996).

CHAPTER 8

1. L. Pervin and O. John, *Personality: Theory and Research*, 8th ed. (New York: John Wiley & Sons, Inc., 2001).

2. David Augsburger, *Sustaining Love: Healing & Growth in the Passages of Marriage* (Ventura, CA: Regal Books, 1988), 1–31.

3. P. Costa and R. McCrae, "Bibliography for the Revised NEO Personality and NEO Five-Factor Inventory" (Psychological Assessment Resources, Lutz, FL, 2003).

4. David Augsburger, 55.

CHAPTER 9

1. John Gottman.

2. Ibid.

CHAPTER 10

1. Neil Clark Warren, *The Triumphant Marriage* (Colorado Springs, CO: Focus on the Family, 1995), 105.

2. Special thanks go to Phil Perkins, Fire Management Officer, Yellowstone National Park, for his contributions to this chapter.

3. Information on the Yellowstone wildfire of 1988 can be found online at *www.nps.gov/yell/nature/index.htm*.

4. John Gottman.

5. Diane Sollee, "What's the Number One Predictor of Divorce?" *www.smartmarriages.com/divorcepredictor.html*.

6. Warren, 105.

CHAPTER 11

1. D. H. Olson and A. K. Olson, *Empowering Couples: Building on*

Your Strengths (Minneapolis: Life Innovations, Inc., 2000).

2. Harriet Lerner, *The Dance of Anger* (New York: Harper and Row, 1985).

3. H. Markman, S. Stanley, and S. Blumberg, *Fighting for Your Marriage: Positive Steps for Preventing Divorce and Preserving a Lasting Love*, rev. ed. (San Francisco: Jossey-Bass, 2001).

CHAPTER 13

1. Patricia Schiff Estess, *Money Advice for Your Successful Remarriage* (ASJA Press: Lincoln, NE, 2001), 6.

2. M. Arond and S. L. Pauker, *The First Year of Marriage* (New York: Warner Books, 1987).

3. Estess, 6–8.

4. Ibid., 86.

5. M. Coleman and L. Ganong, "Financial management in stepfamilies," *Journal of Family and Economic Issues*, 10, (1989) 217–232.

CHAPTER 14

1. Barry and Emily McCarthy, *Couple Sexual Awareness* (Cambridge, MA: Da Capo Press, 2002).

2. We appreciate Dr. Sytsma's contributions to this chapter. Find more from Dr. Sytsma at *www.intimatemarriage.org*.

3. Barry and Emily McCarthy.

4. Douglas Rosenau, Michael Sytsma, & Debra Taylor, "Sexual Desire and Frequency," in Douglas Rosenau, *A Celebration of Sex: A Guide to Enjoying God's Gift of Sexual Intimacy* (Nashville: Thomas Nelson, 2002).

5. We recommend *A Celebration of Sex* by Dr. Douglas Rosenau (Thomas Nelson Publishers, 2002) or *The Way to Love Your Wife* by Clifford and Joyce Penner (Tyndale House Publishers, 2007).

6. D. Taylor and M. Sytsma, "7 things you need to know about sex," *Marriage Partnership* magazine (Summer 2007).

7. A. D. Hart, C. H. Weber, and D. Taylor, *Secrets of Eve: Understand the Mystery of Female Sexuality* (Nashville, TN: Word, 1998).

8. C. McCluskey and R. McCluskey, *When Two Become One: Enhancing Sexual Intimacy in Marriage* (Grand Rapids, MI: Revell, 2004).

9. This suggestion comes from Clifford and Joyce Penner, *The Way to Love Your Wife.*

10. McCluskey and McCluskey.

11. E. D. Moreira, G. Brock, D. B. Glasser, et al., "Help-seeking behavior for sexual problems: The global study of sexual attitudes and behaviors" *International Journal of Clinical Practice,* 59, no. 1, (2005) 6–16.

12. Find a listing of Certified Christian Sex Therapists at *www.abcst .org.*

CHAPTER 15

1. John DeFrain and David Olson, *Marriages & Families: Intimacy, Diversity, and Strengths,* 5th ed. (New York: McGraw Hill, 2006), 74.

2. G. H. Gallup and D. M. Lindsay, *Surveying the Religious Landscape: Trends in U.S. Beliefs* (Harrisburg, PA: Morehouse Publishing, 1999).

3. See J. DeFrain and N. Stinnett, "Family strengths" in J. J. Ponzetti, et. al. (eds.), *International Encyclopedia of Marriage and Family,* 2nd ed. (New York: Macmillan Reference Group, 2002); and Nick Stinnett, Nancy Stinnett, Joe Beam, and Alice Beam, *Fantastic Families: 6 Proven Steps to Building a Strong Family* (West Monroe, LA: Howard Publishing, 1999).

4. A. Mahoney, K. I. Pargament, N. Tarakeshwar, and A.B. Swank, "Religion in the home in the 1980s and 1990s: A meta-analytic review and conceptual analysis of links between religion, marriage, and parenting" *Journal of Family Psychology,* 15, no. 4 (2001), 559–596.

5. P. J. Larson and D. H. Olson, "Spiritual beliefs and marriage: A national survey based on ENRICH." *The Family Psychologist,* 20, no. 2 (2004), 4–8.

6. S. Stanley, D. Trathen, S. McCain, and M. Bryan, *A Lasting Promise: A Christian Guide to Fighting for Your Marriage* (San Francisco: Jossey-Bass Publishers, 1998), 261.

7. Donald Harvey, *The Spiritually Intimate Marriage* (Grand Rapids, MI: Chosen Books, 1991).

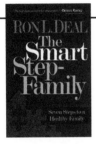
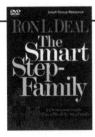